{ hand made walls }

22 inspiring ideas
to bring your walls to life

Jamin + Ashley Mills, thehandmadehome.net

A **adams**media
Avon, Massachusetts

Published by
Adams Media, a division of F+W Media, Inc.
57 Littlefield Street, Avon, MA 02322. U.S.A.
www.adamsmedia.com

ISBN 10: 1-4405-7232-1
ISBN 13: 978-1-4405-7232-6

Printed in the United States of America.

10 9 8 7 6 5 4 3 2 1

Library of Congress Cataloging-in-Publication Data

Mills, Jamin.
  Handmade Walls : 22 Inspiring Ideas to Bring Your Walls to Life / Jamin + Ashley Mills, thehandmadehome.net.
      pages cm
  ISBN-13: 978-1-4405-7232-6 (pbk.)
  ISBN-10: 1-4405-7232-1 (pbk.)
1. Picture frames and framing. 2. Pictures in interior decoration. I. Mills, Ashley. II. Title.
  TT899.2.M55 2013
  749'.7--dc23
                    2013031063

Readers are urged to take all appropriate precautions before undertaking any how-to task. Always read and follow instructions and safety warnings for all tools and materials, and call in a professional if the task stretches your abilities too far. Although every effort has been made to provide the best possible information in this book, neither the publisher nor the author is responsible for accidents, injuries, or damage incurred as a result of tasks undertaken by readers. This book is not a substitute for professional services.

Photos courtesy of Jamin and Ashley Mills with the exception of the Polariod backdrops used throughout the book, which are provided by and used with permission from Fuzzimo.com.

Cover image © Jamin and Ashley Mills.

This book is available at quantity discounts for bulk purchases.
For information, please call 1-800-289-0963.

{ hand *made* walls }

For Aiden, Emerson + Malone
You are the ultimate inspiration.

For our incredible readers
You are why we do what we do.

Thank You.

We have so many people to thank. So many people have inspired, enriched, and supported our journey, not only in this book but in our growth as writers and creatives. This doesn't even scratch the surface, but how do we begin to find the words in which to express our overwhelming appreciation?

- -

To our parents: The power that comes from believing in someone and supporting them is absolutely invaluable. Even if our creativity may have scared you a little at times, you have been there for every step anyway. We hope to be half the inspiration to our children as you have been to us.

To (Ashley's) parents: Having your involvement in this means the world to us. You are the best cheerleaders and editors we could ask for. From those fifth grade English papers through those moments of delirium and tears, you've been there. You are truly an endless blessing to our entire family. Thank you.

To Myquillyn: Thank you a million times over for being a real catalyst. For finding our blog that first time and inspiring us to pursue this in more ways than you know. For encouraging us and supporting us, grateful doesn't begin to cover it.

To Andrea: For being our sounding board over the years, thank you. We know we can be ridiculous. Thank you for listening to our rants and raves and crazy ideas. Thank you for all your hard work with this book. You've done more than you realize and are a forever friend.

To Tony: You have been just as much a part of this journey as we have, and we're only at the beginning. You are like family to us. What would we do without you?

To Layla + Shaunna: Thank you for inspiring and pushing us, in more ways than you probably know, to write this book. To pursue it. For encouraging us to go all the way fearlessly, we thank you.

To Erin: You are one person we're thrilled to call our friend. Thank you for your time and feedback. You're a real, genuine treasure.

To Mitch: For your time, effort, wisdom, and patience in helping us launch this and so many other projects. You have been so good to us, and we are endlessly indebted.

To our wonderful network of countless inspiring, amazingly talented blogger friends and affiliates: Wow. We couldn't do this without you. Thank you so much for your camaraderie. It's truly priceless.

And last but certainly not least, to our readers: You continue to floor us with your love and support. We are completely wowed daily by your kindness. You've transformed us. Thank you.

{ *table of*
contents }

foreword

I can still remember the very first time I laid eyes on Ashley's home. I stumbled onto her blog and there was a photo of her enclosed porch with the aqua and white striped siding walls and collage of chunky frames holding black and white photos of her children. I heard an audible gasp and realized that it came from my own lips. There are a handful of people in this world whose style I truly envy, and Ashley is one of them.

Her home was layered and storied and meaningful, the kind of home every child would be lucky to grow up in, the kind of home any adult would love to come home to at the end of the day. I couldn't stop looking at it. I left inspired and motivated. And I feel the same way about this book.

For anyone who's ever wished their home could be more unique, more personal, more custom-without-the-fuss, Ashley and Jamin have put together a beautiful collection of handmade ideas for your walls. Ideas that will add meaningful beauty to your home—you know the stuff you'd grab if your house were on fire and your husband and kids and dogs were out and you had five minutes to make a mad dash and grab some things you love? It's this stuff, this beautiful, meaningful art that you will learn how to create in this book that helps make the transition from house to home.

You're gonna wish you had more walls.

Myquillyn Smith
The Nester
www.thenester.com

introduction

When we purchased our first home, we were overwhelmed.

While we both grew into a passion for decorating our home, we were frustrated with the lack of translation from the pages of pretty, glossy magazines and our own unrealistic expectations. Things just didn't feel like 'us.' We were frustrated with the limitations from the big box stores with their small range of options and the impossible to reach, to the trade conundrum which plagued our satisfaction as homeowners. And we were tired. Tired of overthinking. Tired of seeing the exact same items from our home, everywhere. We wanted our home to feel unique. To feel like us. It was as if we were searching

for our design voice to build a home for our family, but weren't sure where to find it. We craved something different and struggled with how to translate our creativity into our home. Most of all, we were exasperated with the seemingly ridiculous prices we saw cropping up everywhere. We had mouths to feed, and wanted to enjoy our lives. We didn't like the idea of being slaves to overpriced, overused, impractically overplayed purchases. We wanted to try new things. We wanted to take risks but weren't sure where to start. So we stayed stagnant with what was 'accepted.'

As artists and creatives to the core,
we had a love for creating,
but weren't sure how to make that translate
from the canvas to the home.

Frustration can be a good thing.
It forced us to look for a solution.
And from that struggle, we grew.

Our handmade home started with the walls.

With our nine-month-old son, we stood there, transfixed. We'd stopped by a little store while on vacation, and were staring at a mass-produced frame we'd spied in the back. The price tag glared back at us with a stiff two hundred and seventy five. Dollars. We knew exactly where said frame would go, and if we were honest, we kind of wanted three. At the time, we simply didn't have the funds or the justification for something so seemingly over the top. Jamin's mom, who was standing there with us, shot a sideways glance and murmured, "You could make that, you know." That simple statement sparked a fire in our bones. Putting our heads together, we decided to build something.

We came to the realization that after all this time, the one thing that had been holding us back on changing our home over to something we both loved was simply our fear and our own inhibitions. Stopping us were our own thoughts of what we'd initially believed our home was 'supposed' to be. We wanted to paint our (perfectly fine, though strongly disliked) kitchen cabinets white, but we worried about the future homeowners. Wasn't that going against 'the rules'? We wanted a lighter sofa to make up for eager beaver shoppers' remorse, but worried it was a bit dramatic to get rid of our perfectly good, leather bachelor's pad statement for something we really wanted.

And then it dawned on us. Why were we waiting to enjoy our home? What if we never had the chance to 'do that in our next house'? What if there wasn't ever another house? Why were we living in the future? And whose preconceived notions were we listening to anyway? They were a collection of silly thoughts, entertained by us.

A switch was flipped and we both started to think differently. We went through a 'rebellious' stage of all things home. When we built a wall on our back porch for extra square footage, and finally changed our perfectly good (cookie cutter nightmare) cabinets to a beautiful white farmhouse look, we wondered why it had taken us so long to enjoy our home. From there, it began. We threw out our inhibitions and preconceived notions. Who cared about what our future homeowner's sister's aunt might think about our choices? We stopped playing the comparison game. We stopped worrying.

In the process of creating things for our home, we found that we left a stamp, or a personal touch, on each project we made. When we did that, each creation was an extension of us. Our home began to feel more like ours. We were fearless in our choices, and in creating the things we loved. We both stopped listening to that silly inner voice. And only then did we truly begin to love our home.

Our philosophy
behind what we do is plain + simple

In the process of creating pieces
for your home, a transformation occurs.

In both you and your lovely abode.

You leave a personal impression . . .
a mark, if you will, on each project.

With each piece, you lose a little fear.
And gain a little bravery.

Each creation is an extension of you.
With every piece you create,
you make your home yours.

If your home is literally a piece of you . . .
uniquely yours,
how can you not help but love it?

When you finally let go, the possibilities are endless.

What we want you to take away.

Please know that we are in no way experts. We want this book to be simple, and fun to use. If you've never built anything a day in your life, it's all about the baby steps. Any processes you see here, we simply learned on the fly and along the way. The idea behind it is this: If we can learn, we hope you feel inspired to as well. This book is written as a building process in itself. You'll find that we start with the basics and, for lack of a better analogy, build on top of that. Once you create one project, you'll find the next a bit easier, and so on.

If you're a weekend warrior, an avid DIYer, or a newbie just wanting to try something different for your home, it is our sincerest hope that within the pages of this book you find inspiration. If you're looking for your voice or maybe even a springboard from which to make your house a home, if you wish to make your home more of a reflection of you, we hope that you find something you love, let go of your fears, and, most importantly, love the home you create.

We hope you fall in love with your home and the possibilities for beauty that lie within.

where to start

how to use this book

{ chapter
one }

how to use
this book

1

You'll find the projects in this book divided by sections.

Frames, Art, + Function: the ways you'll find this book categorized.

This keeps them all organized and in place for you to easily find. We also named our projects. From Lucy and Gemma to Harry and Cooper, we felt their personalities warranted their own names.

4

Project reference guide.

In our final chapter, you'll find our project reference guide. There, you'll find a recap chock-full of painting and cutting tips, tools, and colors we love, and a full-fledged supplies glossary to reference any tools or painting processes you may have had any questions about.

Be sure to check out this section before proceeding with any of the plans in this book. You'll find valuable information there.

supplies *glossary*

our favorite paint **colors.**

*tips + tricks

Some of the tried and true tips + tricks we like to use with each project. Consider it a great chance to learn from our mistakes!

2

More bang for your buck.

One of the main goals of this book was to keep things completely affordable for our wonderful readers. The average cost for each project is around 35 dollars. Just remember, you can adjust any of the materials in this book for your project to fit your price needs.

3

An (easy breezy) learning curve.

Like any sewing book with multiple patterns, our handmade plans build on basic skill levels as you go. So even if you've never built anything a day in your life, have no fear. We won't start with some ridiculous, multifaceted project.

We begin with a little learning curve and it's our hope that this book has something in it for everyone on every level. With a little practice you'll be whipping out the coolest little creations in no time.

This little graphic will be handy on each project. It will tell you at a glance a little about difficulty, time, and price of the project you're about to tackle.

While these are merely guesstimates (it was difficult to be exact based on location and experience) they can be used as a fun little guide.

- Difficulty: 1–5. 1 = As easy as layering or a few simple cuts. (A walk in the park.) 5 = Gain a little experience before tackling this project. (We really don't want you pulling your hair out. Your hair is pretty.)

- Time: A guesstimate of the time this project will take in hours. (Does not include drying time for paint.)

- Price: Each $ symbol stands for 50 dollar increments.

Stella

difficulty · time · price

| 1 | 2 | $ |

With a distinctive look similar to Lucy, Stella holds a grander feel and an ability to showcase memories of a broader spectrum.

Each project contains three main elements: 1. A small reference to visually determine the work needed for each plan. 2. A materials + cut list. 3. Fully illustrated guides to easily make your own, or use as a springboard for your one-of-a-kind wonderful ideas.

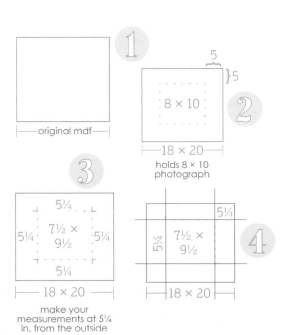

1

original mdf

2

5 }5

8 × 10

18 × 20

holds 8 × 10 photograph

3

5¼

5¼ 7½ × 9½ 5¼

5¼

18 × 20

make your measurements at 5¼ in. from the outside

4

5¼

5¼ 7½ × 9½

18 × 20

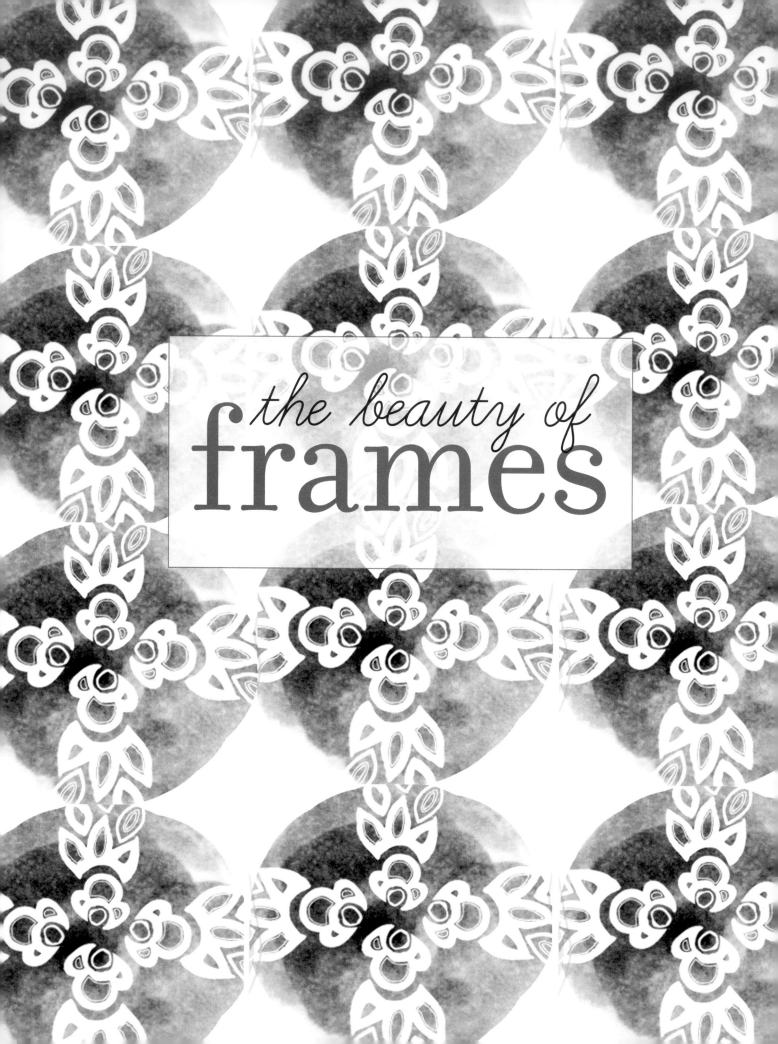

the beauty of
frames

{chapter two}

simply beautiful:
frames

Frames.

The most basic of all home decor, frames
are the easiest way to bring instant life to
your walls. They are the best place to start
with handmade creations, and they serve
as a complement to your already existing
masterpieces. Whether it's showcasing a
simple photograph or a creation by a child,
from galleries of beautiful collections to a
simple understated elegance, frames can
be a stunning addition to your space. In that
singular display of handmade beauty . . . This
is the best place to begin with the basics.

In the process of creating pieces for your home, a *transformation* occurs.

Francis

A simple overlay with plenty of pizzazz, Francis, in many forms, makes for the perfect addition.

Where there's a drill, there's a way. No, we couldn't resist.

Francis consists of two main parts, and with the help of your local home improvement store requires no real cutting on your part. This is the perfect place to begin if you don't have any experience with tools of any kind.

Francis is probably one of the best places to start when it comes to frames and construction if you've never made anything before. You can have the assistants at your local store cut the main pieces for you.

The perfect place to begin.

From vintage paper to children's art, pressed flowers, and anything else you can think of to hang, any wall is transformed into an instant gallery. This great little display makes the perfect showcasing creation anywhere in your home.

This basic overlay frame, for us, captures the epitome of creating for the home. A one-of-a-kind piece like Francis makes ordinary, everyday objects an inspiring collection to behold.

Francis

difficulty	time	price
1	**2**	**$**

With two pieces that can be pre-cut by local distributors, Francis is the perfect place to begin.

the Francis frame

> Materials

Backing Materials of Your Choice
Here you'll see we used both layered MDF (Medium Density Fiberboard) and stained wood to create the backbone of this piece. The resulting look is ultimately up to you.

Plexiglas
Cut to at least 2 inches smaller than your backing material.

Drill + Drill Bits

#6 • ½-Inch Screws (4)

Tips + Tricks

* Francis makes the perfect frame as a starting point. It requires absolutely no cutting on your part. However, if you wish to start practicing here, it's the best place to begin.

* Did you know? The helpful people at your local home improvement store will provide outside cuts for you, free of charge.

* It's also cheaper, and a way to get more bang for your buck, to purchase Plexiglas from your local glass company. You only buy what you need rather than large sheets. They cut it down to size for you.

* If you decide to stain your wood, we encourage you to go with a pre-stain wood conditioner. It helps prevent blotchy finishes later.

* Plexiglas usually comes with a protective paper, and if you have problems with the adhesive backing we recommend Goo Gone and a quick spritz with window cleaner. Problems are rare, but this should help.

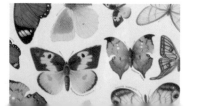

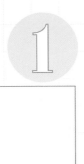

Deciding on the overall look of your frame, begin with how large you want your piece to be with either MDF or wood. We start with thinking about what we might use our frames for and build around that. We allow at least 2 inches greater in the size of our backing material to make for a generous border.

Remember that the helpful people at your local home improvement store will provide outside cuts for you free of charge.

├── cut to size ──┤

If you're staining a block of wood, begin with wood conditioner to avoid any problems with the finish. Some wood has a tendency to streak and blotch over time with its stain. This helps prevent that. When that dries, apply your stain. If you're using MDF, apply the painting treatment of your choice.

Once your piece is dry, line up your Plexiglas with your block of wood. If you've had it cut at the local store, it's best to make it at least 2 inches smaller than the original backing piece for a great border around your frame.

Most Plexiglas comes covered in a protective paper, so leave it on until you're ready to apply it in the final step.

Measure out ¼ of an inch on all four corners, from all four sides of your Plexiglas. Use your drill and a drill bit (at a width that suits your screws) to drill into the plastic.

Eyeball (or measure) the Plexiglas centered over the backing piece you've already painted. Use a pen to mark the holes you've already drilled in the Plexiglas. Remove the Plexiglas and drill the holes into your backing piece.

Place the art of your choice over your backing piece, and place your Plexiglas (unwrapped) over the art. Using your four screws, screw them into place. Make sure they are secured in each corner.

Tada! You're officially finito with your first ever piece!

the francis frame

1. Francis serves as a wonderful, one-of-a-kind creation for any space and a great display for a versatile array of choices. For the finish you see here on our block of wood, we first used wood conditioner and topped it off with Minwax's Early American.

2. For the MDF version, we used a darker blue/green undertone in mixed paints from what we had around our home. Once it was dry, we coated it with a lighter blue. (Try Behr's Adriatic Mist for the perfect shade of aqua.) We then lightly sanded it down in various areas and in different directions. Finally, to bring out the deeper tones and brush strokes, we wiped it down with some stain on a rag (and followed behind lightly removing). It made a great tea-stain topper in Minwax's Early American.

3. For a great tea-stained look, we recommend you literally use the wipe-on, wipe-off method. It's touch and go in multiple directions until you have the look you wish to achieve. A sponge brush is great for establishing that first coat, and anything like an old rag or paper towel works for wiping off excess. Simply wipe away quickly before it starts to dry. Repeat this to achieve whatever level of darkness you wish.

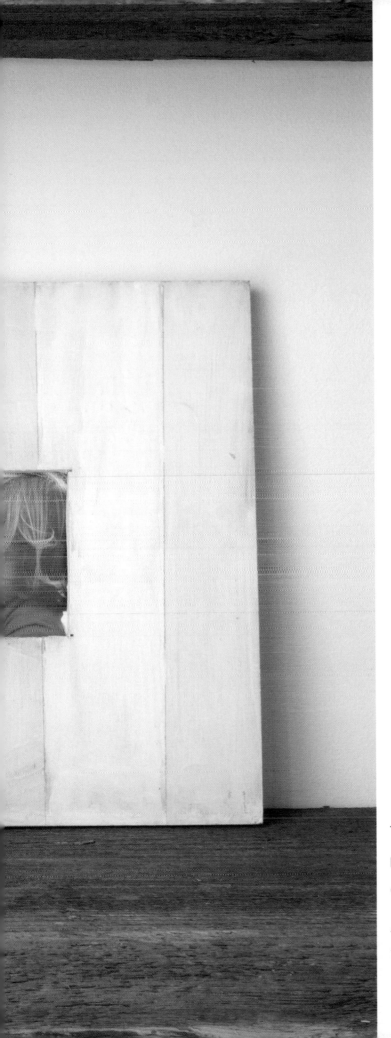

Lucy

The basic
rectangle frame shows us its
elegant diversity . . .

And transformative power in
the home.

The DIY version of creating your own frames is not only the beginning of a different look for your home.

It opens up an entirely new, generous array of options for those who want something fun and unique. A change from the usual.

Starting with the basics: What shape is brought to mind when the word "frame" is mentioned?

When beginning the entire process of building traditional frames, we felt it best to start with the original and most basic of shapes. If you can tackle Lucy, you're well on your way to conquering anything, mastering basic measurements and construction. This shape (along with the simple square) will serve as a springboard from which our designs in the frames department originate. So here, we'll dive right in with the basics. A simple rectangle. As you

The simplest of shapes make for great, versatile displays.

can see here, this shape can serve a variety of purposes. As picture frames to display simple objects or command centers made from metal and fabric backing, there's a spectrum of options with what you can do. The simple rectangle is a great shape to build upon, as you'll see with later projects.

Lucy

difficulty	time	price
1	**2**	**$**

Starting with easy-to-cut MDF, this simple design stays simple + affordable.

the Lucy frame

breaking it down:

> Materials

MDF

For this frame, our material of choice is MDF. For this project we purchased a 2 × 4 sheet at ½-inch thick.

Chalk Line

Makes measuring those straight lines a real cinch. We recommend blue chalk, as it rubs off easily and is not permanent.

Skilsaw

Every basic cut you see in this book will be made with this saw.

Jig Saw

This saw will certainly come in handy for the detailed cuts.

Painting Materials of Your Choice

Tips + Tricks

❋ Always remember that your handy-dandy local hardware store will be more than happy to cut the original piece for you, for free. They do not do inside cuts, but they will do the overall outside cuts for your frames. Simply starting out with the purchased piece at the right size is an easy beginning.

❋ Don't forget your 'display allowance.' Your innermost frame's dimensions will always be a little less than the actual photo you plan to hold.

❋ Your chalk line is your new friend in terms of measurements, and most saws come equipped with a laser guide. Use that guide to help you line up with your measurements.

❋ You can use photo corners on the back of your frame or even simple tape to display your product of choice. If you want, use a drill to make it a leaning frame with a simple dowel in the back. Otherwise, hang with a basic picture-hanging kit.

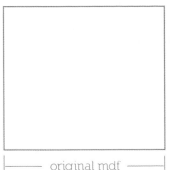

original mdf

First things first: Decide how large a photo you want your finished frame to hold. We'll be using an 8 × 10 photograph as an example.

8 × 10

18 × 20

holds 8 × 10 photograph

From there, determine the overall (outer) dimensions of the frame. This will be the border that surrounds your innermost opening for the photograph itself. In our example, we will use 5 inches on all sides.

You will then add 10 inches (5 + 5 because you are doing 5 inches all the way around).

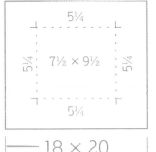

5¼

5¼ 7½ × 9½ 5¼

5¼

18 × 20

make your measurements at
5¼ inches from the outside

This is your width + height. This will give you your overall frame size. For our example, it would be 8 + 5 + 5 = 18 and 10 + 5 + 5 = 20. So our frame will be 18 × 20.

With our newly cut wood at 18 × 20 inches, we would begin marking out our inner dimensions for cutting. A very important rule to remember when it comes to displays for frames: Even though the photo is 8 × 10, the innermost rectangle for photograph display will need to measure 7½ × 9½ (¼ inch both sides = ½). We leave what we like to refer to as a 'display allowance' at ¼ inch. With that in mind, measure in from each side: 5¼ inch, to make up for the display allowance (extra ¼ inch).

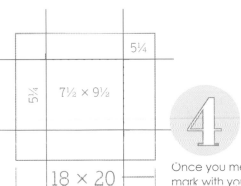

5¼

5¼ 7½ × 9½

18 × 20

Once you measure in, place a mark with your pencil. Do this for all four corners. Don't forget both sides of each corner. Once you are finished measuring and marking there should be 8 marks, 2 for each corner. Think of them as crop marks. Double-check your measurements.

Use your chalk line to stretch across, snap, and mark your spot. Do this on all four corners.

When you are finished, there should then be a blue box in the center of your wood. Cut it out.

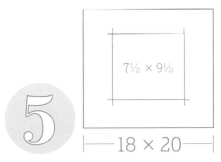

7½ × 9½

18 × 20

Take your Skilsaw, and line the blade and the guide line (this is the dash on the front part of the blade guard) to cut on your pretty blue line. Then raise up the blade and engage the motor. Once your blade is running, bring it back down on the blue line. Cut the length of the line, and stop just short of the corner. Repeat on all four sides. Once you are done with the Skilsaw, it's time to break out the jig saw. Cut out the remainder of the corners by following what is left of the blue line. (Be careful after you've cut two corners. The center piece may want to fall out.)

When you're finished cutting and the centerpiece has popped out, flip it over. This is the side you will most likely use. You're ready to paint, so finish your design as you choose and adhere your art or photo to the frame.

the Lucy *frame*

If you completed this simple frame, congratulate your-self on a job well done. You've made something com-pletely unique for your home!

1 When mounting it to the wall, we use a basic picture-hanging kit attached to the back. If you prefer for your frames to be freestanding, always consider using a drill and short dowel as an option. A small hole and dowel in the back will allow it to lean freely.

2 For this particular finish, we gave the frame a coat of Behr's Magnolia Blossom. When that layer was dry we established stripes with two contrasting colors: Behr's Asparagus + Adriatic Mist. Finishing it off with a light tea stain in Minwax's Early American should give your frame a similar look.

3 Simple hanging tip: In a series, frames look better closer together than farther apart. Keep the ratio of wall in between each frame smaller, with less space in between than around them. When hanging them above furniture, we like to keep them at eye level with minimum space in between for the best display.

4 This frame makes a fun, simple addition to display love-lies in your home. Enjoy!

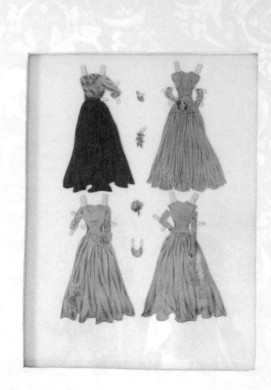

Stella

Stella is a simple throwback to Lucy on a grander scale, with a little bit of glitz and polish.

Used to display
memory-worthy
art, or even antique
keepsakes, Stella is a
unique creation for
any space.

We consider Stella a mini springboard throwback from Lucy. With the addition of Plexiglas, this frame can sturdily hold a variety of items.

From larger keepsakes like art and posters, to tiny memorabilia displayed in a large memory box on the wall, Stella opens up a new array of possibilities.

Stella serves as a grand display with a subtle polish.

You can adjust this frame from the thickness of its borders to its painting treatments. Whether Stella is made in a strong geometric pattern with bold colors or organic and soft with light and bright, you can use it as a floating or classic design. In this larger version of Lucy, Stella's creative composition is up to you.

Stella

difficulty	time	price
1	**2**	**$**

With a distinctive look similar to Lucy, Stella holds a grander feel and an ability to showcase memories of a broader spectrum.

the Stella frame

breaking it down:

> ## Materials

MDF

The frames you see here measure at 26 × 32 and 34 × 40 both with inside dimensions of 17 × 23 inches. Purchase your MDF at a size of 2 × 4 feet for one frame. For multiple frames, 4 × 8 feet. We recommend once again using the ½-inch thickness.

Chalk Line

Skil + Jig Saws

Plexiglas

Depending on what you plan to display, one or two pieces cut a bit larger than the actual opening on your frame.

Cardboard

This will be used as your backing, if you don't use the floating frame option.

#6 • ½-Inch Screws (10)

Painting Materials of Your Choice

Tips + Tricks

* Stella is basically a larger version of Lucy. Adjust its borders and colors to give it a varying degree of uniqueness.

* You can obtain Plexiglas at your local glass store for a much lower price than big hardware stores.

* We recommend for all larger frames mentioned in this book that deal with MDF, going with the thinner ½-inch thickness.

* When joining your Plexiglas to the MDF, be careful not to screw it in too tight to avoid cracking the glass.

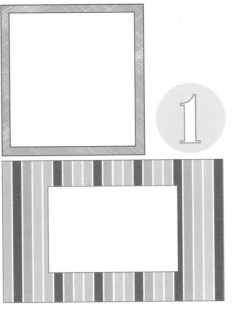

For the first half of these plans, you'll simply follow the basic Lucy frame layout adjusted to your size preferences.

Depending on your wishes for the ultimate outcome, you can go with a larger thickness for added drama, or thin on all sides for a modern simplified look. A variety of finishes can keep it interesting. While we included our own dimensions on the materials list for reference, you can use any size measurements you desire.

1

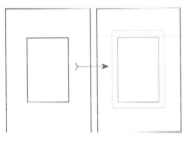

Flipping your finished frame over, you'll take the Plexiglas (cut to a slightly larger size than the display of the frame) and place it over the opening. Place your art behind it and top it off with a piece of protective cardboard. If you decide on a 'floating' look, place your item face down, then cover with another piece of Plexiglas. We recommend securing it with tape to the back of the second piece of Plexiglas so it doesn't shift.

2

3

To join your layers of art and Plexiglas to the frame, overlap at least ten of your screws onto the frame with the Plexiglas. This should securely hold the Plexiglas to the back. Remember that depending on your desired finish, if you're not going for the floating look as seen with the paper dolls you can always use butcher paper to hide your backing. Be cautious as you apply the screws. You don't want too much pressure to crack the glass. When it begins to resist, that should do the trick.

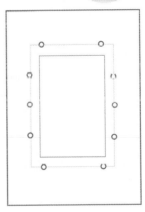

To hang your artwork, you have two choices. Either attach a picture-hanging kit or, if the materials on the back are too thick, nail right through the frame and into the wall on all four corners for an industrial look. Try to attach these to a wall anchor or stud to help keep your frames safe and secure. Enjoy your new creation!

4

the Stella frame

1 A larger, slightly glamorous and more versatile version of Lucy, Stella makes a great frame with sturdy capabilities.

2 If you go for the floating look with this frame, be sure to use a piece of double-sided tape behind each item for reinforcement to avoid shifting. If a traditional look is in order, be sure to use some cardboard to cushion the back of your Plexiglas. This will protect it from scratching or cracking when securing it with screws and help hold your item in place.

3 For the striped finish you see to the left, we started with a base coat of Benjamin Moore's Chantilly Lace. Once the first layer was dry, deciding on what we wanted our stripes' widths to be, we taped them each one at a time. We simply pushed the blue (Behr's Adriatic Mist) to the line without actually touching it to leave the white exposed underneath. This gives it a bit of that 'tie-dyed' appearance in the final finish.

4 For more details on our painting techniques, be sure to check out the last chapter for our Project Reference Guide.

Iris

A double take on the Lucy frame, this sophisticated sister adds a simple step with a lot of pretty flair.

Layers and punches of color add instant interest and handmade spark to any space.

With a multitude of patterns, ideas, and you as the creative, the promise for beautiful creations is never-ending.

One look at Iris, and you'll know that the leap between this frame and Lucy is not a vast one. The difference is one simple, extra step.

The best part is you can mix + match these pieces throughout your home to create diversity and beauty for your handmade walls.

A creation by you, to display the prettiest of pieces.

As an added bonus, Iris is a great frame for those just beginning. The additional layer on top covers a multitude of sins in the cutting department. If you were to over-cut on your inside edges, no one will even know. So if you're just starting out on your handmade journey, this frame is a great place to begin.

Iris

difficulty	time	price
1	2	$

Starting with easy-to-cut MDF and topping frame, this is one way to give those walls a handmade look.

the Iris frame

breaking it down:

▶ Materials

MDF

For this frame, our material of choice is MDF. We recommend purchasing a 2 × 4 sheet. This will be at whatever thickness you choose.

Frame of Your Choice

No. Really. We're cheating with this one, and it will be your topper.

Chalk Line

Makes measuring those straight lines a real cinch.

Skilsaw

Every basic cut will be made with this saw.

Jig Saw

This saw will certainly come in handy for the detailed cuts.

Wood Glue + Hot Glue

Painting Materials of Your Choice

Tips + Tricks

❋ Cheater's alert: Though it's possible to build the mounted section from crown molding cut to an angle (more on that ahead), this frame is composed of two elements: a simple rectangular frame built by you, and a chunky pre-made, repurposed frame positioned on top. These can range anywhere from ridiculously dainty additions to the large and in-charge custom frame shop pieces. You can find them anywhere from your local craft store to thrift shops and antique malls. Simply add a layer of paint if you wish, and you have an entirely different look. That's what makes these frames so delightfully unique. So, deciding how large the piece you want in your soon-to-be-built frame is where you start. (Again, we will use a basic 8 × 10 in our example.)

❋ Measure twice, cut once. Always double-check your measurements. It's a little extra time but it saves you a lot of madness.

❋ Use a combination of both hot and wood glue to temporarily stabilize the frame while it dries permanently.

original mdf

1

First, just as before in our simple frame tutorial, begin with deciding the overall (outer) dimensions of the frame. In other words . . . how large the entire frame will be. Remember from our previous tips, your local hardware store will be glad to cut the outer dimensions for you, for free.

2

Next, measure the outer dimensions of the (found) frame that you plan to mount. The easiest way to do this is lay the found frame face down on top of the existing MDF and measure the underneath side. (In our example, the outermost measurements of the 8 × 10 frame will be 12 × 14.)

Once its measurements are established, decide how much of a border you will want around the mounted frame. (Our example will use 5 inches on all sides.)

Again, it's simple math . . . just the process of thinking through it. Add 10 inches (5 + 5 because you are doing 5 inches all the way around) to the mounted frame size (width and height) and this will give you your overall frame size of 22 × 24.

12 + 5 + 5 = 22
14 + 5 + 5 = 24

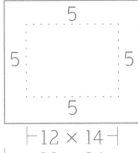

├ 12 × 14 ┤
├ 22 × 24 ┤

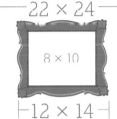

├ 12 × 14 ┤

3

With your newly cut piece, start marking those inner dimensions. You need to measure in from the outer edge of the wood, the 5 inches for the border and also the 2 inches of our mounted frame. 5 + 2 = 7.

Since our mounted frame was conveniently 2 inches on every side, our work is easy. If your mounted frame is not the same all the way around just make sure you measure in 5 inches + whatever that measurement is.

Measuring in, place a mark. Do this for all four corners and don't forget both sides of each corner. Once that is complete, there should be 8 marks, 2 for each corner. Think of them as crop marks.

Double-check your measurements.

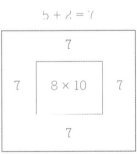

make your measurements
at 7 inches from the outside

4

Use your chalk line to stretch across, snap, and mark your spot. Do this on all four corners.

When finished, there should be a box from your chalk line in the center of your wood. You're now ready to cut.

5

Take your Skilsaw, and line the blade and the guide line (or dash on the front part of the blade guard) to cut on your pretty line. Then raise up the blade and engage the motor. Once your blade is running, bring it back down on the blue line. Cut the length of the line and stop just short of the corner. (Repeat on all sides.)

When you're finito with the Skilsaw, it's time to break out the jig saw. Cut out the remainder of the corners (you can only go so far with a Skilsaw) by following what is left of the blue line. Be careful after you have cut two corners. The center piece may want to fall out.

6

Paint both your newly constructed rectangular shape (using whichever treatment you choose) and your separate piece you intend to mount (if you choose to paint it). When they are dry, simply use wood glue on the back of the mountable frame and place it over the center of the constructed rectangle, right side up. Helpful hint: You can use a hot glue gun for stabilization and combine it with wood glue, if you wish.

├ 22 × 24 ┤

the Iris frame

1 Whether you completed Iris or just enjoyed reading through the process for now, you're one step closer to creating a home you love with handmade walls.

2 When mounting Iris to the wall, we used a simple picture-hanging kit attached to the back. If you're attaching a frame to the front that already has its own 'back' we recommend removing the back on the original frame. You may then insert your photo through the back of the new combined frame. Add a little tape to secure it.

3 Some of these frames include glass, and some do not. Don't sweat it if some of your pieces are different. They blend together nicely on the walls for a great, cohesive look.

4 This frame is also fun to lean on shelving or atop pieces of furniture. The bigger the better with chunky, striking Iris.

Charlie

Charming and absolutely striking in a display, a lot of fun for your home can be found in this simple form.

The second easiest design to make is a square-shaped frame with just a few additional steps. Between Charlie and Lucy, this is one of the basic building blocks for making much more.

With its basic shape and simple construction, Charlie opens up a generous world of possibilities.

From simple layers of stripes and Mod Podged pattern to detailed paintings, you can use these frames in various sizes for just about anything.

A charming statement maker.

For baby's keepsakes, beautiful works of art, or a simple sentimental photograph, these handmade frames are special pieces that are sure to be a conversation starter. And as we know from personal experience, they make amazing gifts, as well.

These versatile frames
can be made in various
sizes, and even the same
concept (above) behind
a different shape.

Charlie

difficulty	time	price
1	2	$

Charlie serves as a charming springboard and a simple composition for more projects ahead.

the Charlie frame

breaking it down:

> Materials

MDF
For this frame, our material of choice is MDF. We recommend purchasing a 2 × 4 sheet to create Charlie, at whatever thickness you choose.

Chalk Line

Skil + Jig Saws

Cork Tile
Found at your local craft store, this will serve as the lightweight 'background' for the floating part of your frame.

Wood Glue + Hot Glue

Painting Materials of Your Choice

Tips + Tricks

While we began with a rectangular shape in Lucy to establish simplicity, basic mathematics rule that the square is the easiest shape of all to work with, simply because it's even on all sides.

When you're ready to attach your cork and middle part of your frame to the actual frame, use wood glue, and then before it's placed, a dab of hot glue. One offers permanence while the other offers temporary stability for drying.

When you're finished cutting, flip your piece over for painting. It's probably the side you will want to use because there will be no obvious blemishes or gashes.

To get that perfect centered look with the square frame, position the final square the photo will sit on in the middle of the cork. Then apply the glue. This gives you the freedom to readjust.

First things first: Decide how large a piece you wish to place in your soon-to-be frame. We'll use a standard 8 × 8 photograph in our example.

Next, determine the negative space you wish to have around the piece before the body of the frame will begin. We will use 2 inches in our example.

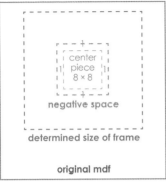

8 (picture size) + 2 (negative space size) + 10 (border size) = 20

Once you have these two measurements (picture size + negative space) you will need to decide how much frame you want around the negative space. In our example, we will use 5 inches on all sides. You will then need to add all your measurements to give you the overall dimensions of your frame. 8 (picture size) + 2 (negative space size) + 5 × 2 (border size) = 20.

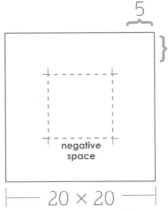

With your newly cut wood at 20 × 20, begin marking out your inner dimensions. Measure in from the outer edge of the MDF, 5 inches for the border.

Once you measure in, place a mark with your pencil. Do this for all four corners. Don't forget both sides of each corner. Once you are finished measuring and marking, there should be 8 marks, 2 for each corner. Think of them as crop marks.

Double-check your measurements.

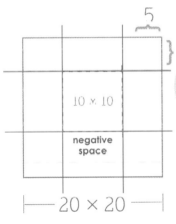

Use your chalk line to stretch across, snap, and mark your spot. Do this on all four corners. After you are finished, there should be a blue box in the center of your wood.

You're ready to cut. Put on your safety gear, and never cut without it.

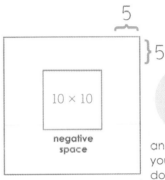

Take your Skilsaw and line the blade and the guide line (or dash on the front part of the blade guard) to cut on your blue line. Then raise up the blade and engage the motor. Once your blade is running, bring it back down on the blue line. Cut the length of the line and stop just short of the corner. Repeat on all four sides. Once you're finished with the Skilsaw, it's time to break out your jig saw. Cut out the remainder of the corners by following what is left of the blue line. (Be careful after you've cut two corners. The center piece may want to fall out.)

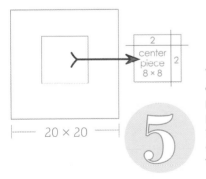

When you're finished cutting and the center piece has popped out, put the actual frame to the side. It's now time to cut the wood block that will hold the picture.

Using the center piece that was just cut from the bigger piece of wood, measure in 2 inches on only two sides. Place marks with your pencil and 'pop' it with the chalk line just as we describe in the supplies glossary. There should only be two lines. Once the lines are popped, cut the wood by following the blue line with your guide.

Assemble + paint: Wipe down the smaller block of wood and the frame you just finished cutting. Breaking out your piece of cork, simply flip the frame over and attach the cork. We like to use a dab of hot glue in each little section, along with wood glue, for security and permanence. Flip it back over and, if you wish, measure and place that centermost piece with more glue. (We like to eyeball and then scoot it around, accordingly!)

Once that glue is dry, paint with the application of your choice and tada! You're finito! You may mount your center photo with photo corners or simple double-sided tape.

the Charlie *frame*

1 Charlie makes a great addition, leaning on any surface or hanging on any wall as fun decor. This frame looks amazing in a series with layered paint and contrasting patterns.

2 To achieve the same finish you see on Charlie, the look is similar to the one you may have spied on Lucy. We painted the outside borders first. For this version, all of Charlie was a dark brown underneath. When the first layer was dry, we used painter's tape and painted every other stripe contrasting colors: Behr's Adriatic Mist + (a color similar to) Benjamin Moore's Once Upon A Time. Instead of taking each stripe all the way to the line, we removed the tape after the stripe was established and pushed all the color to one side. This way, the brown peeks through, giving it that great rustic look.

3 We used double-sided tape to mount all the photos in these square frames to the center MDF. It makes for an easy change and simple switcharoos. We find that photos look best in this frame, with a simple white border. It offers an additional element of interest and that extra pop.

4 From here you'll see the basic building block that is the simple square come to life, while applying this model to new ideas we'll see ahead.

Henley

Henley is a bit like the second generation of Charlie. With varying looks and one-of-a-kind finishes, it's a gorgeous display for any space.

Give it uneven borders (above) for a chunkier look and watch as it becomes a real anchoring fixture in your space.

A variety of patterns with endless choices are a great finish for this frame. Layers + texture add real interest.

Henley makes a striking display and an amazing show-stopper for any wall.

This simple frame holds three pieces and makes a huge impact with pattern, texture, and even layers. It's an empty canvas for you, the artist, to create and then display your latest and greatest in a series on your handmade walls.

Positioned vertically or horizontally, Henley is a versatile piece.

Simply think of Henley as a variation of Charlie. Times three.

This frame is relatively simple to create, and with a few extra steps you're well on your way to a well-thought-out one-of-a-kind display for your walls.

Henley

difficulty	time	price
2	2	$

A great springboard from the original Charlie, Henley is a bigger, versatile display of a closely related cousin.

the Henley frame

breaking it down:

> Materials

MDF
For Henley we recommend purchasing a 2 × 4 sheet of MDF, at ½-inch. A thinner MDF makes a larger frame more manageable for your walls.

Chalk Line

Skil + Jig Saws

Cork Tiles (3)
Found at your local craft store, these will serve as the lightweight 'background' for the floating part of your frame.

Wood Glue + Hot Glue

Painting Materials of Your Choice

Tips + Tricks

* For this frame, we recommend a thinner MDF. Henley can be a bit of a charming beast and a challenge to mount on the wall. The lighter the weight, the better.

* When you're finished cutting, flip your piece over for painting. It's probably the side you'll want to use as there will be no obvious blemishes or gashes.

* When you're ready to attach your cork and middle section to the actual frame, use wood glue, then before it's placed use a dab of hot glue. One offers permanence while the other offers temporary stability for drying.

* For that uniform, centered look, paint all three pieces separately. Place the square in the middle of the cork and then apply the glue. This gives you freedom to readjust.

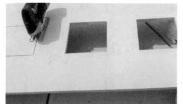

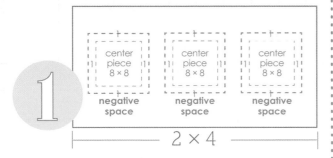

1

With your 2 × 4 piece of MDF at home, you'll need to decide how large you want your photos to be and how much negative space you want around them. For our example, we'll use an 8 × 8–inch picture with 1 inch of negative space on each side.

Lay out your MDF, and break out the pencil and chalk line. Just to clarify, our orientation with measurements for this tutorial: We will use the 2-foot measurement as our height and the 4-foot measurement as our width.

2

The overall width is 48 inches, and you'll need three 10-inch holes on the width. That takes out 30 inches and leaves us with 18 inches of border space. We will have four border spaces. With 18 inches left, and four border spaces, that means we will have 4½ inches for each of our four borders.

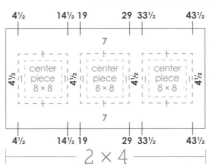

On one of the 2-foot edges, measure in to (do this near the top edge):

4½ inches and place a mark.
14½ inches and place a mark.
19 inches and place a mark.
29 inches and place a mark.
33½ inches and place a mark.
43½ inches and place a mark.

Repeat this process on the bottom.

3

We know the overall height of the MDF is 24 inches and we will have one 10-inch hole. This leaves us with 14 inches of border space, which we will divide by 2 to give us two 7-inch borders.

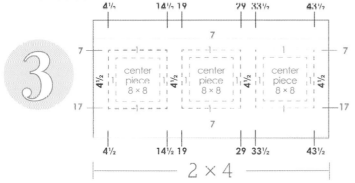

On one of the 4-foot edges, measure in to 7 inches and place a mark + to 17 inches and place a mark. Do this toward the outer edge, and repeat the process on the opposite side.

4

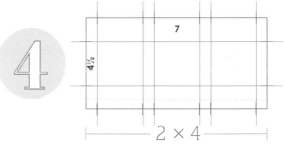

Once you have all your marks, take your chalk line and 'pop' a line. Once you pop all the lines there should be three 10 × 10 boxes with 7 inch borders, or 4½ inch borders, depending on the side. After all three groups of four lines have been popped, you are ready to cut. We recommend wearing some safety gear for that handy dandy Skilsaw.

Line the blade and the guide line (the dash on the front part of the blade guard) on your blue line. Then raise up the blade, engage the motor, and, once your blade is running, bring it back down on the line. Cut the length of the line and stop just short of the corner. (Repeat on all four sides.)

Once you are finished with the Skilsaw, get out your jig saw and cut out the corner by following what is left of the blue line. Be careful after you have cut two corners, as the center piece may want to fall out.

5

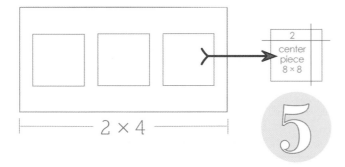

Finally, you'll need to cut the three pieces that will hold the 8 × 8 picture. On the squares that have already been cut from the frame, simply mark 2 inches in from one side twice, and pop a line. Then cut. Repeat this with all three pieces.

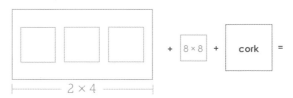

Take your newly cut frame, centerpiece, and cork. Assemble and paint.

6

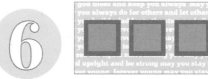

the Henley frame

1 The beauty of Henley is that this frame works both vertically and horizontally. It also looks amazing in a series with layered paint and contrasting patterns.

2 When mounting it to the wall, we use a simple picture-hanging kit attached to the back. Double-sided tape for mounting all the photos in these square frames works best. It makes for an easy change and simple switcharoos.

3 For painting Henley, first we recommend painting all the pieces separately. For the main body, work on the borders and then the front of the frame.

4 To assemble Henley, when the frame is dry, flip it over face down. Using a combination of hot glue and wood glue (temporary and long-term permanence), add your cork tiles. While the cork tiles are secure with the hot glue, flip Henley back over and add your MDF center squares. To make sure they're uniform, use a T-square or simply eyeball each one. Test out each position by placing them on top before you apply the glue. Add the glue underneath and center the squares, placed in the middle of the cork centers.

5 For this particular frame, we used Royal Design Studio's Moroccan Arches All Over Stencil, combined with Benjamin Moore's Chantilly Lace and Silver Satin.

Gemma

Think of Charlie, in multiples. This single most stunning display is all you need to make your space a true masterpiece.

Like all proud parents do, we wanted something practical with an original look to display our children's photos in our home. Of course, we were discouraged by the limited options and prices that were available at the time. We once again decided to make our own, and the idea for Gemma was born.

This gargantuan frame is the perfect choice for any area that needs a little personality. You can transform any room with one statement-making piece. Mounted to the frame with simple double-sided tape, the best part is that you can switch them out as easily as your mind and whim changes. It's like a rotating gallery of your greatest masterpieces. From photos to anything you collect, with Gemma, the simplest of objects becomes an instant work of art.

The ultimate display for whatever you wish.

Gemma can become a smaller . . . or even larger (with additional MDF) version of what you see here.

Gemma

difficulty	time	price
3	**5**	**$$**

Gemma is that amazing display for all your cherished keepsakes and photos that you've been looking for. The best part? Created by you.

the Gemma frame {

> Materials

MDF

For this project, you'll need a 4 × 8 piece of MDF at ½-inch thickness. This is the largest size available. We're simply cutting squares from this shape to turn it into a frame.

Chalk Line

Skil + Jig Saws

Cork Tiles (18)

Cork tiles, by nature, can get expensive quickly. They go on sale regularly at your local craft store. See an alternative suggestion below.

Wood Glue + Hot Glue

Painting Materials of Your Choice

Tips + Tricks

* For this frame, we recommend a thinner MDF. If Henley was a beast, then Gemma ate him. Six times.

* This project will take the help of some extra hands. It's not difficult so much as laborious, and we think you'll be grateful for an extra pair to help with this heavy frame.

* We prefer cork for its lightweight manageability. To save more, you could always use a large piece of plywood on the back to cover all the individual holes.

* As with the rest of our 'floating square' frames, we recommend flipping Gemma over once you've finished cutting all the pieces. Then secure the initial pieces of cork with both hot glue and wood glue for a foolproof construction.

* For hanging: Use caution, especially with children in the house. For ours, rather than using picture-hanging kits, we put nails in each corner and an additional one in each side straight through and into the wall. That's six secured nails. It hasn't budged.

Your local hardware store sells MDF already cut in a 4 × 8 size. We personally prefer the ½-inch thickness. Remembering that your local hardware store will cut your original piece for free, have them cut your MDF down to 95 inches. This will make the math much easier.

Decide how large you want your photo to be, and how much negative space you want around it. We're working with 8 × 8 pictures + 1 inch of negative space on each side. Lay out your MDF, and break out your pencil and chalk line.

Just to clarify our orientation with measurements for this tutorial: We will use the 4-foot measurement as our height, and the 8-foot measurement as our width.

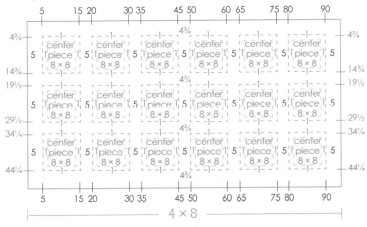

4 × 8

What we know: Our overall width is 95 inches (since we actually had it cut down a little). We will need three rows of six 10 × 10 holes to contain our eighteen 8 × 8 pictures.

Thinking first about the width (the 95-inches-across side): We need six 10-inch holes. This will give us seven border spaces. Since our six holes will take 60 inches (10 × 6 = 60), it will leave us with 35 inches, which will need to be divided by 7. This will leave us with 5-inch borders.

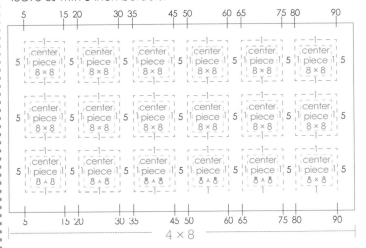

4 × 8

 On one of the 4-foot edges, measure in to (do this near the top edge):

5 inches and place a mark.

15 inches, 20 inches, 30 inches, 35 inches, 45 inches, 50 inches, 60 inches, 65 inches, 75 inches, 80 inches, and 90 inches. Place a mark each time. Repeat on the bottom.

 We know the overall height of the MDF is 49 inches. (Yes, we know 12 × 4 = 48, but the good people that make MDF for us are generously official, and always give us a little extra.) We'll have three 10-inch holes. This leaves us with 19 inches of border space, which we will divide by 4, to give us four 4¾-inch borders.

From one of the 95-inch edges, measure up 4¾ inches, and place a mark toward the outer edge. On the same 95-inch edge, measure up to:

14¾ inches, 19½ inches, 29½ inches, 34¼ inches, and 44¼ inches. Place a mark each time. Repeat the process on the opposite side.

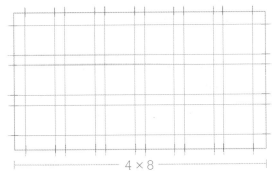

4 × 8

 Once you have all your marks, take your chalk line and 'pop' a line. Once you pop all the lines, there should be eighteen 10 × 10 boxes, with 5-inch borders. Or 4¾-inch borders, depending on the side.

After all of the lines have been popped, you are ready to cut. With your Skilsaw line the blade and the guide line (the dash on the front part of the blade guard) on your blue line. Then raise up the blade, engage the motor, and, once your blade is running, bring it back down on the line. Cut the length of the line and stop just short of the corner. (Repeat on all four sides.)

Once you are done with the Skilsaw, get out your jig saw and cut out the corner by following what is left of the blue line. Be careful after you have cut two corners. The center piece may want to fall out.

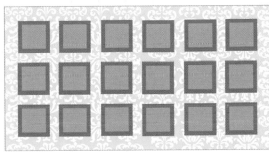

Finally, you will need to cut the pieces that will hold the 8 × 8 photograph. Simply mark 2 inches in from one side twice, and pop a line. Then cut, as described above. This should give you one 8 × 8 piece of wood. Repeat this step with all eighteen pieces.

Assemble + paint: Wipe down the smaller blocks of wood, and the frame you just finished cutting. We determine the front after we cut, based on which side looks the best. Break out your pieces of cork and simply flip the frame over (perhaps with the help of a second pair of hands) to attach the cork pieces. We like to use a dab of hot glue in each little section, along with wood glue, for security and permanence. Flip it back over and place the centermost piece with more glue. We like to eyeball and then scoot it around, accordingly.

Depending on what you're more comfortable with, this piece may be easier to paint once it's all put together, simply because of the sheer number of pieces. Once the glue is dry, paint with the application of your choice and tada! You're finito!

the Gemma *frame*

1 The beauty of the Gemma frame is that not only does it make an amazing display, but you can shrink or even enlarge the basic idea, to build any size you like.

2 We recommend cork tiles or squares because they're easy to work with and weigh less. But to save more, you could always use a large piece of thin wood.

3 Simple hanging tip: We recommend using nails through the frame and into a stud, or some type of wall anchor. One in each corner, and then one on each side for safe and secure holding.

4 Once it's hung with nails, simply go back and touch up with whatever paint you originally used on your frame. Or leave it exposed for an industrial look.

5 We use double-sided tape to mount all the photos in these square frames to the center MDF. It makes for easy change and simple switcharoos.

6 We find that photos with a simple white border look best in this frame. It offers an additional element of interest and that simple pop.

Darby

Moving on from MDF as our primary material, these simple, angled frames are a fun take on a traditional look.

These fun, chunky, angled frames are a great beginning to amazing, one-of-a-kind handmade walls in your home.

A basic look with a lot of fun, the Darby frame is a great combination when used with vivid colors and unexpected contrasts.

A bold take on a traditional

While the basic cut of a 45-degree angle is the same concept you spy in our trim frames around our home (shown here), the main Darby designs are made with simple, fat pieces of wood.

Bold colors and bright contrasts with fun lines and interesting combinations add beauty and handmade flair when brought into a space.

frame makes them an instant classic.

Instant beauty is found in the unexpected contrast of stain and paint together. Bold colors abound.

Darby

difficulty	time	price
③	②	$

With simple, stained planks of wood joined together and a unifying splash of paint, these pieces are sure to become an instant favorite.

the Darby frame

breaking it down:

> Materials

1 × 6 × 6 Wood

Corner Vise/Clamps

Corner Brackets (4)

Wood Glue + Hot Glue

Sandpaper

Painting Materials of Your Choice

Miter Box + Hand Saw (or Miter Saw)

In lieu of working with a miter box or miter saw, a carpenter square will help you measure out those perfect angles.

Carpenter Square

Butcher Paper or Felt (Optional)

Tips + Tricks

*   Angled frames can be tricky with their seams, so don't expect absolute perfection the first time around. Practice makes perfect.

*   Wood filler can help with those imperfect seams. If you want the stained look, try stain + paint with a little wood filler in between covered by paint to hide any mess-ups. (See our blue Darby for the general idea.)

*   If you wish to use a stain to finish it off, be wary of your wood glue. It can leave a trace behind. Just be careful when applying it, and wipe off excess.

*   If you have a nail gun at your disposal, we say go for it. These frames could easily be put together at an angle with a nail gun. The point of these plans is to offer the simplest, most affordable option. So to finish it off we recommend using corner brackets or vise grips.

*   For a more finished look on the back, once the photo has been placed, simply cover it in butcher paper or felt to hide any unwanted areas. Attach a basic picture-hanging kit and it's complete.

As always, you will need to decide how big you want the frame to be. With this frame, you'll need to not only think about your picture size (we will use a 5 × 7) but also consider the size of the boards you wish to use to make the frame. They will determine the size frame you can create. (For example, let's say I want to use 1 × 6 pieces of wood, which are actually about 5½ inches in width. This means my frame size would be 16 (w) × 18 (l). 5½ × 2 gives you 11.)

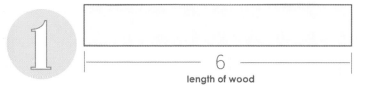

6
length of wood

Once you determine your size, it's off to the local hardware store to buy some wood. You will need to add up all the sides to know how much wood you will need. For example, in our piece, the length would need to be 68 inches, or 6 feet. (18 × 2 = 36 plus 16 × 2 = 32, which = 68.) Note: In step two, the size will actually shrink a little bit, so that the photo behind the frame will be supported.

Consider buying a little extra (one 8-foot piece). You will also need to buy a miter box and hand saw, if you don't own a miter saw.

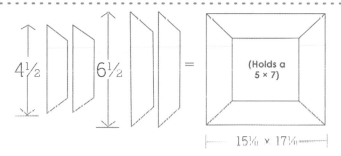

4½   6½   =   (Holds a 5 × 7)

15½ × 17½

Take all four pieces you have cut, and begin placing them together. You may need to trim or sand them a little to adjust, and make them fit snugly.

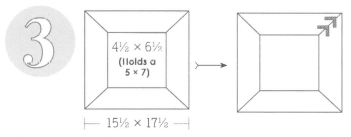

3

4½ × 6½
(Holds a 5 × 7)

15½ × 17½

Once you have them together, you have two options. We recommend simple corner brackets to join the wood together. But if you have a nail gun or corner vise and wish to use it, this will be your next step.

For the vise: Place the pieces in the vise and glue them together. If you do use a vise to glue them together, make sure you use some sort of corner bracket or other stabilizing piece to secure the frame. Glue will not hold on its own. The downside to vises are their price, so we included an alternative. If you do not own a vise, then follow the next step.

For the corner brackets: You will need to spread some glue along the cut edges of the pieces you are about to join. We like Gorilla Wood Glue. Have one person hold the pieces together tightly as you screw a corner bracket into place.

Once home with the wood, let the cutting begin. First, mark out your inside pieces. This should be (two) 7-inch, and (two) 5-inch pieces. (Note: We suggest you cut it short ¼ inch on both sides for your display allowance. This will leave you some wood to mount the picture from behind once it's complete. If you do this, then your cut would be at 6½ inches and 4½ inches.)

When cutting along a line, always remember that if you cut right on the line you will end up cutting your board a little shorter than you mean to. You have to adjust for the width of your blade. The easiest way to fix this: Always line up your blade on the outside of the line.

The mark you made is going to be the inside, or bottom mark. In other words, you will cut away from the mark leaving a top piece that is longer than your mark. If you choose to use a carpenter's square, feel free to utilize it to help you measure out the perfect angle and cut along the line that it gives you.

To cut, place the wood in the miter box or saw. You will be making a 45-degree angle cut. (Again make sure that you cut in such a way that the longer side is on the top, not the place that you marked.) Repeat this on each side, with all four pieces.

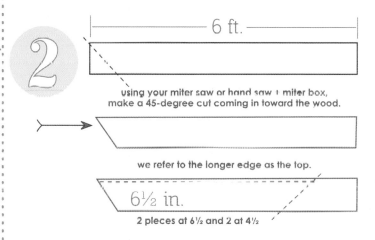

6 ft.

using your miter saw or hand saw + miter box, make a 45-degree cut coming in toward the wood.

we refer to the longer edge as the top.

6½ in.

2 pieces at 6½ and 2 at 4½

Once you've assembled your frame and the glue is dry, decide on your painting treatment and go for it with your awesome mad design skills. Patterns over stain are a wonderful combination with this frame.

If you wish to have a more 'polished' look on the back to cover your corner brackets, place your photo securely with tape or photo corners, and then cover it with butcher paper cut to size. Just realize you will have to remove the butcher paper any time you wish to replace the photo.

the Darby frame

1. With the varying thicknesses and options behind Darby, the possibilities are endless for your handmade walls.

2. We recommend using Minwax's Wood Conditioner before applying any type of stain to the wood of your choice. To apply, use a paper towel or rag, smooth it on evenly, and allow it to dry. Then apply your stain. This helps avoid that potential blotchy look later.

3. For the look you see to the left, we simply applied the wood conditioner. Once it was dry, we used Minwax's English Chestnut. 1. For the blue: Benjamin Moore's Calypso Blue roughly brushed on leaving a few places bare to show the stain beneath. We then topped it off with more stain and our tea-stain look on top for an even richer tone. 2. For the yellow: Benjamin Moore's Corn Husk on stripes created with tape.

4. For more details on specific finishes, be sure to check out the back of our book for painting techniques.

Thatcher

An extra step added to the simple Darby frame can make a big difference in those distinctive looks for your handmade walls.

Whether it's wood or MDF, with all the different choices for trim, the smallest difference will completely change this look.

The colors alone make this frame an excellent, versatile, easily blendable, and classic piece for your handmade walls.

Thatcher is a polished gentleman . . . Like adding a bow tie to your suit, this frame is the next pretty version in a different look for your handmade walls.

The basic idea behind Thatcher is that this frame is Lucy (the MDF rectangular frame) or Darby (the angled frame in the previous plans) with a simple step added.

A simple second step for a super polished look.

Whether it's a traditional trim, a simple plank of wood, or a fun detailed piece, this frame looks great with all the different options behind it.

You'll begin to see that all the frames in this book are mix + match and blend well together in a great, fun look on your handmade walls.

Thatcher

difficulty	time	price
3	2	$

One simple step added on to the typical composition of a basic frame adds a polished touch and a classic look.

the Thatcher frame

breaking it down:

Materials

Materials

1 × 6 × 6 Wood

Trim of Your Choice

Here, we used quarter round trim cut to size. Any smaller piece of trim will do. Remember to stay thin for your display allowance.

Corner Vise/Clamps

Corner Brackets (4)

Wood Glue + Hot Glue

Miter Box + Hand Saw (or Miter Saw)

Sandpaper

Painting Materials of Your Choice

Carpenter Square

Butcher Paper or Felt (Optional)

Tips + Tricks

Don't expect absolute perfection with this piece. It's the little imperfections that make it so charming.

Wood filler can help with those imperfect seams. This works best with paint as the finish, but can also be done with a paint-and-stain combo.

On angled frames, when cutting along a line always remember that if you cut right on the line, you will end up cutting your board a little shorter than you mean to. You have to adjust for the width of your blade. The easiest way to fix this: Always line up your blade on the outside of the line.

Thatcher is basically the Lucy + Darby frames, with one extra step. You could also transform some ready-made, store-bought frames into Thatcher by following the steps here.

You'll use a combination of hot glue and wood glue to offer both a secure bonding and permanence for the inside of this frame. Simply add your photo from the back once the frame is complete.

1 For this tutorial, follow the steps for Lucy or Darby in the earlier plans. The supply list that you spy to the left contains all the materials needed for this. MDF (material used in the Lucy frame) can possess a modern look, but is also easily layered and treated with paint for an older, timeless piece. Wood (the Darby frame) requires a few more steps with angled pieces, but can have a beautiful undertone of stains. Be sure to check out these two plans and begin with them so you may add the next steps for your frame to be 'finished' into Thatcher.

Once you've completed the first part of your frame, according to the Lucy or Darby plans, begin the process of adding your trim. The trim alone can completely change the look of your frame: This simple step will polish off your look.

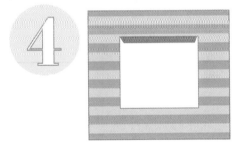

completed frame

2

+ trim } 4

Measure the inside of your frame, for both length and width. Generously pre-cut four basic pieces that you know will be long enough for the inside of your frame.

Making sure the pieces are long enough to fit, measure and cut each piece of trim at a 45-degree angle. Do this on both ends on all four pieces. Cheater's tip: Double-check your measurements by laying each piece over your already made frame as you cut. This helps ensure they will fit. Set each piece aside and number as you go. This way, you're not confused later.

Once each piece is cut, begin to place them on the inside of the frame. Make sure they fit correctly before the final stage of gluing them in place. You may have to lightly sand the angles to ensure a correct fit. Go ahead and paint your trim to your desired finish.

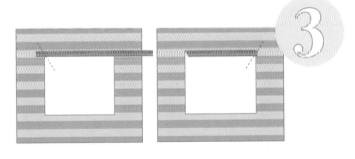

3

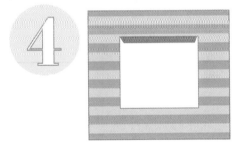

4

5

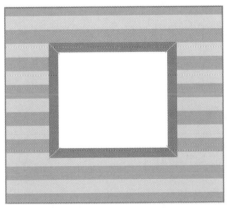

Once you're sure your finished inner pieces will make a nice secure fit, paint your pieces separately and let them dry. Flip the frame over and lay it face down on a protective surface. This will ensure that your pieces are flush with the front of the frame. Placing a thin strip of wood glue on your trim, push it into the open section, and slowly add additional pieces following the same steps. Once you adjust the pieces and make sure they're straight, secure their positions in the frame by adding hot glue to the back for a permanent fixture. Add those finishing touches, like a photograph, and then butcher paper to the back to give it a cleaner, polished look.

the Thatcher frame

1 The versatility and possibilities of finishes behind this polished frame add to the beauty of what you're able to create for your home. Think of Thatcher as a finished version of Darby or Lucy. You can even finish off a pre-fab frame by polishing it up with these simple plans for the Thatcher look.

2 For the stripes on the finished version of Thatcher that you see here, first condition your wood. Once you put your first layer of stain down, simply use painter's tape to mark off each area. For an even spacing between each piece of tape, place an additional (temporary) piece of tape in between each one. Wood has a natural tendency to absorb the stain so that it spreads out. Apply the stain carefully with a small brush, and when it's dry, use a blade (an X-ACTO knife works wonders) to lightly eliminate any imperfections. Just gently scrape any bleeding areas away.

3 For more details on specific finishes, be sure to check out the back of our book for painting techniques.

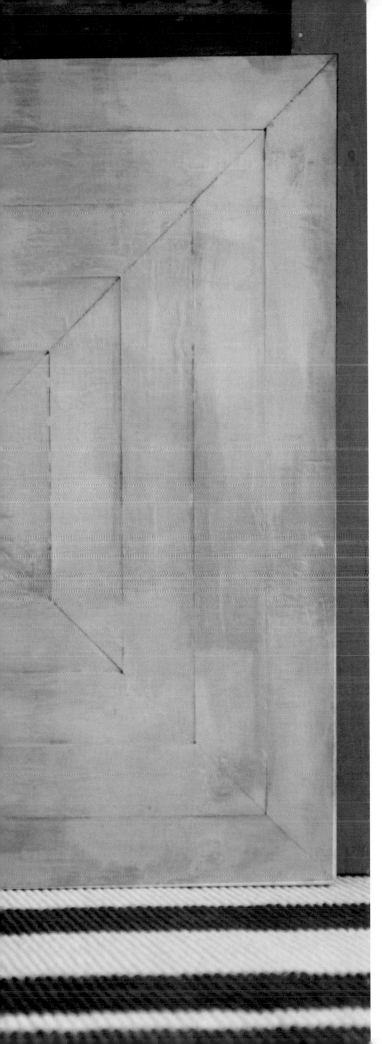

Stanley

Composed of layers of planks for beautiful texture and treated with an array of paint, Stanley has a story to tell all on its own.

Stanley's potential is completely limitless. Widen the display for larger photos, or alter the design with various sizes of wood planks. The choices are up to you.

To say that Stanley makes an interesting handmade piece would be a definite understatement. An uncommon addition with layers of wood planks and textured colors, this is a project that can be well worth taking the time to make.

From the novice to the pro, it's a basic woodworking classic with uniform 45-degree angles on the repeat. Whether it's a nursery, main living area, or kitchen this frame will adorn, Stanley makes a defining addition to any space.

The Stanley frame is a work of art, all on its own.

Stanley can be finished with a spectrum of paint treatments. With layers of varied stain or mottled smudges of color and contrast for a timeless vintage appeal, you're creating beautiful pieces to be handed down for years to come.

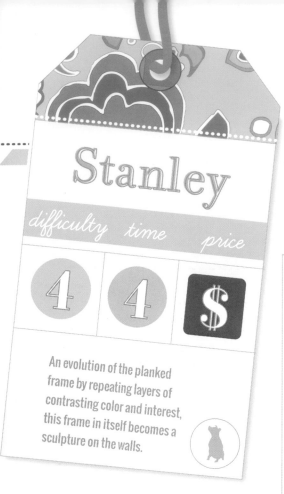

Stanley

difficulty	time	price
4	4	$

An evolution of the planked frame by repeating layers of contrasting color and interest, this frame in itself becomes a sculpture on the walls.

the Stanley frame }

breaking it down:

> Materials

1 × 3 × 8 Wood (4)

Corner Vise/Clamps

Corner Brackets (20)

Miter Box + Hand Saw (or Miter Saw)

Wood Glue + Hot Glue

Sandpaper

Painting Materials of Your Choice

Carpenter Square

Butcher Paper or Felt (Optional)

Tips + Tricks

* The difficulty level for this frame is a 4, but the process is basic. It just requires a little finesse and patience. Looking at the composition of Stanley, you may see that this frame is basically a skinny Darby, on repeat.

* We recommend numbering each piece as you cut, and making sure they fit together properly. This makes for a smoother transition from cutting to placing together later.

* Wood filler can help with those imperfect seams. This works best with paint as the finish, but can also be done with a paint-and-stain combo.

* In lieu of a vise, please note that you can use hot glue to form a temporary bond, while your wood glue dries.

* For a more finished look on the back, once the photo has been placed simply cover it in butcher paper or felt to hide any unwanted areas. Attach a basic picture-hanging kit, and you're done.

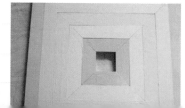

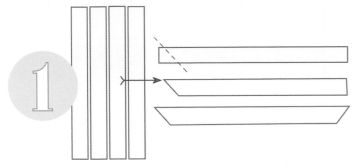

1

The Stanley frame pictured contains a 3½-inch opening for a 4 × 4 photograph, and measures a total of 28½ × 28½ inches. Remember that you can alter this frame to fit your own preference. Gathering your wood, use your miter box or saw and cut four pieces (for each length) at a 45-degree angle on each end. This will have the long edge at the following lengths: 8½, 13½, 18½, 23½, and 28½.

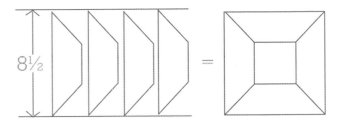

2

When you've completed your cuts, you should have twenty pieces total, at four per square. Before permanently placing your pieces together, sand all the edges to create a smooth fit. Place them together to test their fit.

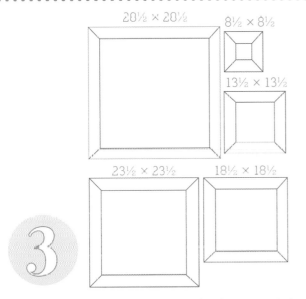

3

To put this frame together, we begin with the separate layers. Spread a little glue on the ends and join them together. Secure them with corner brackets. Repeat this with all four corners on all five layers.

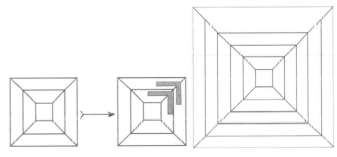

4

Glue all the layers together. Start with the inner and the next largest layer. Spread a little glue on all four edges and use a vise or bracket to hold them together. You can also use a few drops of hot glue as a temporary holder. Repeat this on all layers.

5

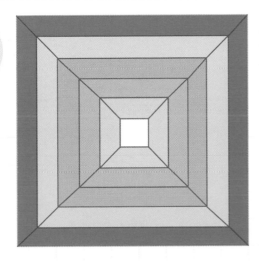

Finish off your frame with any paint color or stain of your choice. For this frame, we used separate colors with each layer that worked in the same tones of a color group. We then took a universal white (Benjamin Moore's Chantilly Lace) and painted a thin layer on top of all the planks. This unified all the layers. When it was almost dry, we rubbed it away in some areas for an aged look. Once completely dry, we then used a rag and some stain and added a thin tea stain on top with Minwax's Early American. This gave it a protective coating and a timeless, slightly aged look, with instant character for a handsome frame.

When it's dry, simply add a photo to the back. You can also cover the entire back with butcher paper once the photo is secure to hide any unsightly areas. Attach a basic picture-hanging kit, and enjoy!

the Stanley frame

1 Stanley offers a handsome option for handmade walls as a piece chock-full of character for any space.

2 Measure twice, cut once. Stanley is the same step, repeated multiple times to create this layered frame. It's not a difficult frame to make, but requires a little diligence and patience.

3 When building Stanley, you can use either corner brackets or a vise. If you decide to use the corner brackets, an extra pair of hands keeps those pieces at a correct angle when assembling. With corner brackets in place, simply mark them. Then drill your holes separately before screwing in the screws.

4 Stanley's size can be altered to accommodate any design. A larger display area for your photo and thicker planks open up a variety of options. This frame can make a beautiful composition on any wall.

5 For more details on specific finishes, be sure to check out the back of our book for painting techniques.

Wills

A frame with two options: Compact and simple or open and breezy, the Wills frame adds an architectural look to any space.

As we've discussed earlier in our book, each frame and project build off one another in various ways. It keeps the construction of hand-made walls attainable, and we hope you've noticed the intentional learning curve with repeated techniques that come with each one.

Wills is like an open version of Stanley, which is an evolved design of Thatcher, which is a polished variation of Darby . . .

One frame.

These concepts continue to build on one another. Even if you've never made anything before, we hope you're beginning to see that hand-made walls and a one-of-a-kind home are affordable and realistically attainable.

Two ways. Endless possibilities.

The beauty behind Wills is that you can keep going with this great open look, or choose the refined and simple composition. Stagger your creations in different ways around the home for fun combinations on your walls.

difficulty · time · price

3 · **2** · **$**

Wills is an elegant frame with numerous variations and great possibilities.

the Wills frame

breaking it down:

> Materials

MDF

For this project, a scrap piece or 2 × 4 sheet will work to create Wills. A ½-inch thickness is the best fit for this frame.

1 × 2 × 8 Wood (6)

Corner Brackets (16)

Box of #6 • 1½-Inch Screws

Miter Box or Saw

Sandpaper

Wood Glue + Hot Glue

Tips + Tricks

※ Wills holds a 5 × 5 photo, and measures a total of 34½ inches, making a grand display in any home.

※ If you decide not to use a corner vise when creating this frame, an extra pair of hands is always helpful.

※ If you wish to use a stain to finish it, be wary of your wood glue, as it can leave a splotchy look behind. Just be careful when applying it, and wipe any extra residue immediately.

※ For this particular frame, we find it best to condition and stain before assembling, if you plan to use stain.

※ For a more finished look on the back, once the photo has been placed, simply cover it in butcher paper or felt to hide any unwanted areas. Attach a basic picture-hanging kit and you're done.

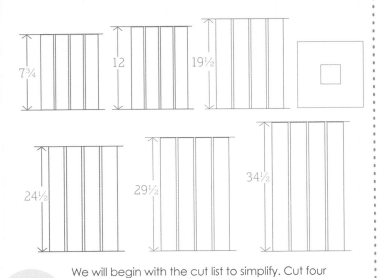

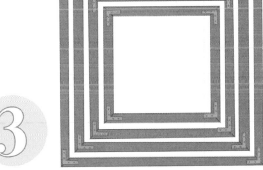

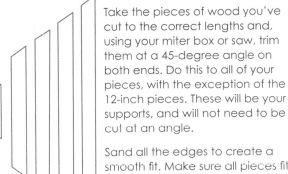

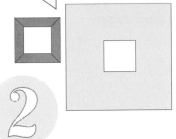

Take the pieces of wood you've cut to the correct lengths and, using your miter box or saw, trim them at a 45-degree angle on both ends. Do this to all of your pieces, with the exception of the 12-inch pieces. These will be your supports, and will not need to be cut at an angle.

Sand all the edges to create a smooth fit. Make sure all pieces fit together securely with their appropriate lengths. Then paint or stain all pieces to a desired finish.

1 We will begin with the cut list to simplify. Cut four pieces each of the following lengths (in inches): 7¾, 12, 19½, 24½, 29½, 34½. Also cut a piece of MDF 16½ × 16½. Then cut a hole in the MDF at a 5¼ × 5¼ size (See the Lucy frame for instructions on how to do this.)

Please note: If you do the simpler version of this frame, the only pieces you will need to cut are the MDF and the 7¾-inch + 19½-inch wood.

2

3 Spread a little wood glue on the 19½ ends of wood and place them together. Secure them with corner brackets. Repeat this on the 24½, 29½, and 34½ layers.

4 Lay the MDF face down. Beginning with the 19½-inch piece, place the layers face down around the MDF. Leave a 1-inch gap between each layer, except on the 19½ layer and MDF, which will be flush.

If you have trouble fitting your MDF, sand lightly one edge at a time until it has a smooth fit.

Center a 12-inch 1 × 2 on all four sides and screw it into each layer using your 1½-inch screws.

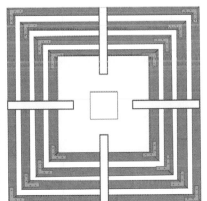

5

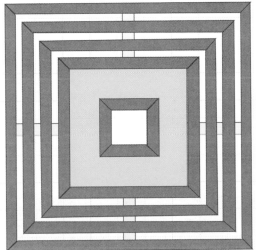

Finally, using wood glue and a few drops of hot glue, secure your final pieces: the 7¾-inch 1 × 2 wood around the hole cut in the center of the MDF. At the lengths and angles cut, they should overlap a bit on the edge for your display allowance. Once you've completed the frame and secured the centermost trim, you're ready to place your photo.

the Wills frame

1. For this frame, we used Minwax's English Chestnut as the stain and Benjamin Moore's Chantilly Lace for the main color of the MDF. We did a quick dry brush with Benjamin Moore's Wedgewood Gray.

2. We recommend having all of your wood cut before you start on the 45-degree angles. This way it's easier to stay organized when a lot of pieces are involved.

3. Remember when cutting your angles that you'll do this to all of your lengths except the 12-inch stack of four, which will be your braces behind the frame.

4. For your back braces, if you know where you'll be hanging Wills, use the same color as the wall for the ultimate floating look. It will camouflage the braces.

5. We use tape or photo corners to mount all the photos in these frames. It makes for an easy change and simple switcharoos.

6. Wills's size can be altered to accommodate any design. This frame will make a beautiful creation for any wall.

7. For more details on specific finishes, be sure to check out the back of our book for painting techniques.

Henry

With layers of contrasting stain and a punch of color, this frame is chock-full of character and a touch of masculine appeal.

Striking features and beautiful finishes create this one-of-a-kind treasure for your home.

This frame makes a simple, yet strong statement for any space.

This versatile, planked frame with a variety of possibilities offers a real punch of personality for your walls. The Henry frame makes It super simple to swap out your latest photograph or masterpiece.

Henry is all about contrast. So whether finished in paint, stain, or both, it works as a beautiful creation for your home and a treasure for years to come.

Henry makes an interesting display and remarkable find.

Henry is a combination of the techniques seen earlier in this book. This frame is joined together by simply gluing pieces of wood to create a unique display solution for your home.

Henry

difficulty	time	price
2	3	$$

Whether stained and masculine or in soft shades of paint with an antiqued stain, Henry is quite the punchy piece.

the Henry frame

breaking it down:

Materials

1 × 2 × 6 Wood (5)

MDF
A ¼-inch thickness 2 × 4 sheet

Box of #6 • 1¼-Inch Screws

Plexiglas (7 × 7)

Corner Brackets (4)

Hot Glue + Wood Glue

1¼-Inch Screw or Bolt of Your Choice (4)

Skilsaw

Tips + Tricks

This frame is a simple combination of techniques introduced earlier in the book.

You can obtain Plexiglas at your local glass store for a much lower price than big hardware stores. They will cut it to size for you.

If you don't have a corner vise, you can use some corner brackets to hold them together until the glue dries, but remember to take them out.

When drilling your Plexiglas make sure to hold it firm so that it doesn't ride up on the drill bit.

If you don't have a corner vise or you don't want to use the bracket method, you can always carefully place the 19½-inch pieces on your MDF and line them up. Just glue them directly to the MDF and spread a little glue between the corner edges.

As always, we begin with our materials and cut list. Cut eleven 1 × 2's to 16½ inches. Cut four 1 × 2's to 19½ inches.

Then cut the four 19½ ends at a 45-degree angle, on all the ends. Sand all of the ends for a smooth fit. Stain or paint your pieces. Cut your MDF (¼-inch thickness) to 16½ × 16½.

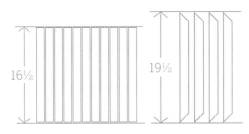

16½

19½

16½

Take your four 19½-inch pieces and glue them end to end using your corner vise and wood glue. (You may opt to use corner brackets here, also.) Once the glue has dried, remember to remove the corner brackets. Glue this piece to the MDF.

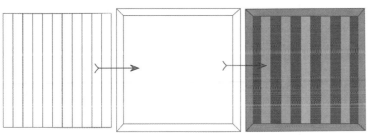

Take your eleven 16½-inch pieces, and line them up as you prefer, on the piece. Spread some wood glue on the MDF in the center of the 19½ frame you just glued down. Then begin placing the 16½-inch pieces on the MDF. Allow enough drying time before painting or staining with your treatment of choice. (See product for specific times.)

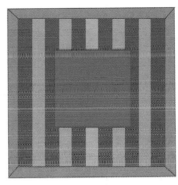

Take your extra MDF left over from step one and cut a 7 × 7 square piece from it. Use your Skilsaw, or saw of your choosing. Stain or paint this piece. When dry, spread a little wood glue on the piece as well as a few drops of hot glue. Attach it to the center of the base. There should be 6¼ inches on all sides from the edge of the 7 × 7 to the edge of the frame.

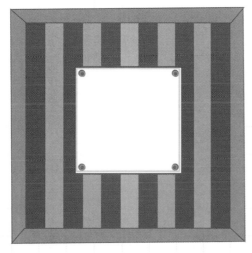

Take your Plexiglas and mark in ¼ inch on each side. There should be 2 marks on each corner. Drill a hole large enough to fit your screw or bolt through.

Place your Plexiglas on the 7 × 7–inch wood and screw it together with the 1¼-inch screws.

Unscrew and secure your object or photo of choice with a simple piece of tape. Reapply your Plexiglas and enjoy!

the Henry frame

1 Henry's photos are simple to attach and change out. Simply stabilize it with double-sided tape and place your Plexiglas with a screw. Henry's planks can be displayed vertically or horizontally on the wall, depending on the frame's orientation. These frames are striking when grouped together in multiples.

2 When building this frame, you can use either corner brackets or a vise. If you decide to use the corner brackets, an extra pair of hands keeps those pieces at a correct angle when assembling.

3 Custom-cut Plexiglas usually comes with protective paper. Simply mark holes in each corner with a little space between the actual hole and the edge. Drill as you go.

4 To create the striped look you see here, initially stain all the planks. Then on every other one, add multiple coats for contrast. In our photos you may notice that some of our pieces were finished before assembly, but our plans show them stained afterwards.

5 For more details on specific finishes, be sure to check out the back of our book for painting techniques.

Harry

A one-of-a-kind design perfect for displaying your loved creations, the Harry frame stands in a class all its own.

Like the vintage sewing cards we all loved as children, these are pretty little jewels for your own unique creations.

With all the different creations in this book, it's hard to pick our favorite design. It really is. But there's just something about the simplicity behind Harry and this great display for all things loved that has us coming back for more.

Whether it's a large masterpiece by a professional artist, or a simple creation that deserves a beautiful display, we think Harry takes the cake.

A beautiful frame for pretty little masterpieces.

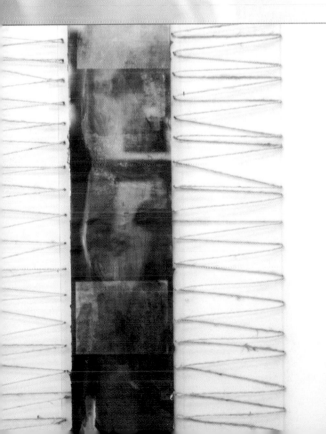

Harry is made from two plain sheets of layered Plexiglas bound together with woven jute. This frame displays any piece proudly.

Harry

difficulty	*time*	*price*
1	**1**	**$**

Harry is a one-of-a-kind creation, and holds artwork beautifully.

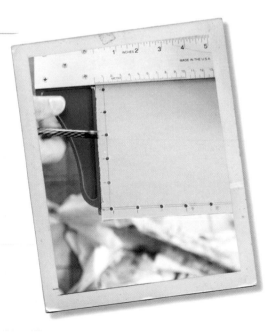

the Harry frame

breaking it down:

> Materials

Plexiglas
Cut two contrasting sizes. Adjust your measurements to make sure there's at least a 1-inch border on the outside piece.

Drill + Drill Bits

Jute
Really, any type of twine will do, but we appreciate that natural element contrasted with that modern, high-gloss, manufactured look.

Tips + Tricks

* You can obtain Plexiglas at your local glass store for a much lower price than big hardware stores.

* When you drill into your measured holes, make sure you hold tightly to your Plexiglas so it doesn't ride up on your drill bit.

* To hang this frame, simply drive a nail through one of the existing holes and into the wall. Hide the nail with your jute.

* When drilling for your jute in these Plexiglas frames, be sure to check the width of your drill bit against your existing jute. Otherwise it can become quite a daunting task.

* For easier threading, try taping the end of your jute to keep it from unraveling as you thread it through each hole.

* If you run out of thread before you're finished, try moving past one hole, securely taping it on the back and out of sight, before starting another.

1 Deciding which art you wish to display is probably a great place to begin with this frame. You can have Plexiglas cut to size for you at your local glass store for much cheaper than your big box hardware stores. Keep your bottom-most Plexiglas size at roughly 2 inches larger on every side.

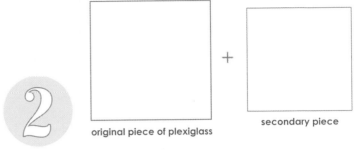

original piece of plexiglass + secondary piece

2 Your secondary piece can be any size. Just make sure it's smaller than the original piece and larger than the piece you wish to hold in the frame. In the larger version you see here, our difference in size created a 5-inch border for a dramatic effect. In the smaller frames, the difference was a 1-inch border.

3 Cut pieces of Plexiglas usually come with a protective coating until they're ready for use. Using this to your advantage, on the smaller Plexiglas piece, measure ¼ of an inch inward. Place your holes 1 inch apart and mark each hole on your smaller piece.

Holding your Plexiglas steady, choose a drill bit that is roughly the same thickness as your jute. Drill out each hole.

When you've finished with your top piece, center it over the larger piece of Plexiglas. Mark each hole so that the two pieces line up.

Remove the smaller piece and drill the same holes in the larger bottom piece.

4 Once your holes are drilled, remove the protective paper from both sides of your Plexiglas. Carefully place your artwork on top of the larger piece that will serve as your backing. We recommend securing it with a piece of tape.

Place the smaller piece over your artwork and larger piece. Line up the holes and begin weaving them together. We recommend using a very long piece of jute. If you run out, simply 'fake it' by finishing out as much as you can, running it past the hole and behind the artwork to tape it in place. Begin your next piece of jute from the exact same spot and simply pick up where you left off. This gives the illusion of one large, continuous piece of jute.

the Harry frame

1 Harry is best used when the artwork is stabilized with a piece of small tape between the artwork and the larger or backing piece of Plexiglas.

2 Make sure you use a drill bit as thick as, if not a bit thicker than, the appropriate measurement for the jute or yarn you plan to use.

3 We find that when threading jute (which naturally wants to split), sealing the end with tape helps it move smoothly through each hole.

4 Make sure you use the protective paper that comes on each piece of cut Plexiglas to your advantage and do not remove it until you're finished drilling the holes. Remember to remove your paper and place your artwork before you begin weaving. If you have problems with the adhesive backing, we recommend Goo Gone and a quick spritz with window cleaner. Problems are rare, but this should help.

5 Once you've lined up your holes on the top and marked the holes on the bottom piece, make sure you don't turn your Plexiglas when you lay it down. When you're ready to replace it on top, lining up the two sets of measured holes is much easier.

one-of-a-kind
art

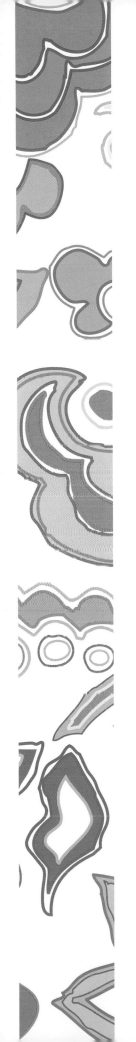

chapter
{three}

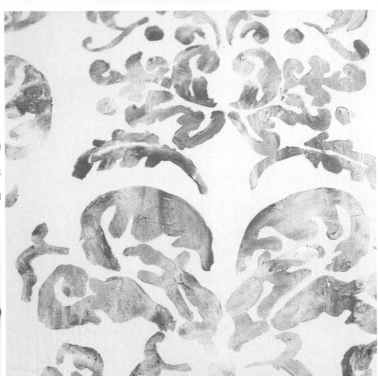

one-of-a-kind
art

Art.

A word that can easily strike fear in anyone's heart who feels that they are not equipped to create something that is considered worthy of 'the title.' But that is the beauty of art. It is so personal, as it comes from within the original creator. It's so genuine and therefore objective that anyone can create it. In that process of creating, a piece of the creator is left behind, inspiring everyone who lays their eyes on it.

You leave a personal impression ... a *mark,* **if you will ... on each project.**

Dalton

A simple slice with an intricate pattern makes a big impact.

Dalton proudly plays the role of a priceless heirloom in your home with layers of beauty that tell an incredible story.

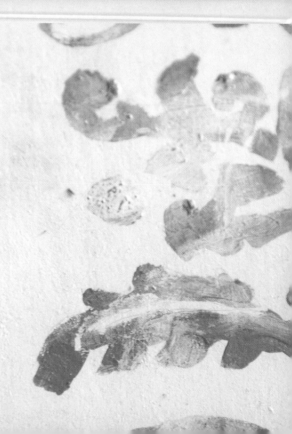

Dalton is a simple piece that can be created with any scrap, pre-cut wood, or MDF from your local hardware store.

The beauty of Dalton's look is that it can be created from any pattern you can find, whether it's a stencil or a design you use from a projector.

Dalton brings aged character to any space.

The secret is the carefully layered painting treatment, which will give any piece you decide to paint a timeless feel and look.

Dalton

difficulty	time	price
2	**4**	**$**

Dalton can be created from any piece of scrap wood or MDF. It only takes a little patience and know-how to create a one-of-a-kind piece of art.

the Dalton creation

breaking it down:

> Materials

MDF (Cut to Size)

Wood is also optional, but Dalton works best with MDF because of its smooth surface. We recommend a 2 × 4 piece. Saw optional.

Overhead Projector + Pattern of Choice

The power of the projector: Though it adds a significant amount of time, it keeps your patterns versatile and possibilities endless. Dalton can also be created with any stencil of your choice. We recommend Royal Design Studio.

Paintbrushes

We recommend at least a typical angled brush to cover large surface areas and a skinny variety to take care of the detailed places.

Paint Colors + Stain

Two contrasting colors and the stain color of your choice.

Paper Towels or Rag

Tips + Tricks

* If you plan to create many projects around your home, we recommend investing in an overhead projector. Though they're nearly extinct, you can find them at most office supply stores and online. They help create accurate lettering, beautiful patterns, and one-of-a-kind looks.

* The beauty of this project is that if you do not have access to an overhead, the painting style will also work with a pattern set in the form of a stencil.

* Dalton is a project that doesn't require a whole lot of skill in the cutting department, but a little patience with painting and the layers that you build up over time.

* You can create your very own version of Dalton, by downloading the provided template on our website: *www.thehandmadehome.net/files/dalton.pdf*. Simply have it printed on a transparency, project, trace + paint! If the provided pattern doesn't cover your entire project area, trace and adjust as you go, continuing your pattern as you proceed. Treat it just like the process of using a stencil for the best coverage.

Beginning with your own predeter-mined size of MDF or scrap wood, apply your base coat. If you have an old can of paint that's getting gloopy, that's even better. We recommend painting in all direc-tions, and even establishing a few layers to build up texture and interest on your piece. This gives it a timeless look.

Once your first coat is dry, set up your overhead and your predeter-mined pattern. We recommend that once you have it straight, tape down your transparency.

Holding your MDF steady, carefully trace your shapes onto your piece.

Once all of your shapes have been established, choosing your second color and a smaller brush, fill in each one with the paint color of your choice. Try to avoid smudges as you go; however, touch-ups can come later.

This step is for the various levels of gradation you see on this project. It's definitely what makes Dalton so fun, if we do say so ourselves. We recommend your fingers as the ultimate tool, and a paper towel or rag for this step. Using your original or base paint color, 'tap' your art to create various levels of cover-age with the lighter color. When it's nearly dry, rub it away in certain areas for a timeworn look.

When that final layer is dry, apply your stain with a rag. Working your way from the outside in, start stain-ing your entire piece to create an older timeless feel for Dalton. With that final layer, you are finito!

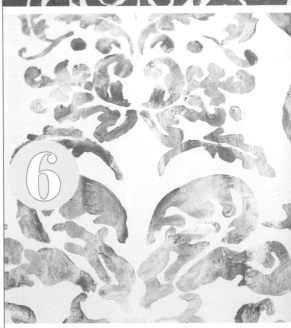

the Dalton creation

1. Dalton creates a timeless, aged feel in your home and will make a striking statement on your wall. This piece looks great displayed anywhere and commands instant attention as a conversation piece for your home.

2. Each layer you paint takes a bit of time, but the more layers you build, the more character you achieve. Consider coating the sides in the same secondary color as your main print for a look of added dimension on the walls. Don't worry about any stray pencil marks when you finish tracing your initial pattern. Simply use your fingers when you come back with the third layer, to touch up any paint or pencil mistakes. Work your stain from the outside in, and once it's placed work quickly to remove it with a rag as you go. Repeat this step as needed.

3. The colors used for the project on the previous pages were Benjamin Moore's Chantilly Lace + Calypso Blue.

Edith

These sweet little letters are like personalized characters for your handmade walls.

These were some of the first pieces we ever made. They were so versatile and easy to reproduce, we were quickly making them for others.

While the idea of a monogram in the home has been trendy for a while, we also think the idea of this presentation is a bit of a classic approach . . . something you can hang as part of a gallery or tuck away on a bookshelf.

Like a pretty little piece of the past adorning your walls.

When it comes to reproducing the look of a letter, fonts are a lot like faces in the world of art. Change one stroke on them, and it's literally back to the drawing board. Our simple approach will help you create pretty, original typography. Edith makes a quiet, unique expression for your home.

These little letters remind us of scattered typewriter keys . . . or something that was once part of an old sign. They make the perfect gift for others . . . or yourself.

Edith

Edith feels like an intimate piece of times gone by with a unique look created and personalized by you. She also makes the perfect gift!

the Edith letter

breaking it down:

 Materials

MDF (Cut to Size)

Wood is also optional, but Edith works best with MDF because of its smooth surface. Cut these to any size you like. Saw optional.

Overhead Projector + Letter of Choice

The power of the projector: Keeps your letters precise. This can also be created by printing a letter out at a larger size, cutting and using it as a template to trace onto your MDF.

Paintbrushes

We recommend at least a typical flat one to cover large surface areas and a skinny variety to take care of the detailed places.

Paint Colors + Stain

Two contrasting colors and the stain color of your choice.

Paper Towels or Rag

Tips + Tricks

* If you plan to create many projects around your home, we recommend investing in an overhead projector. Though nearly 'extinct' you can find them at most office supply stores and online, alongside transparencies. They help create accurate lettering, beautiful patterns, and one-of-a-kind looks.

* If you don't have access to a projector, you can always print out your font of choice in a larger format and cut it to use as your template.

* Just like Dalton, Edith is a project that can be adjusted to any size to fit your spaces. This also makes an excellent gift.

* Consider adding your letter on top of a pattern, such as painted stripes or a stenciled design.

* Fonts used here: Garamond or Filosofia (regular).

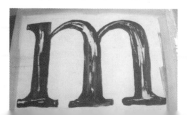

1 Beginning with your own predetermined size of MDF or scrap wood, apply your base coat. If you have an old can of paint that's getting gloopy, this is even better. We recommend painting in all directions, and even establishing a few layers to build up texture and interest on your piece. This gives it a timeless look.

Once your first coat is dry, set up your overhead and your letter. We recommend making sure it's straight, and then securing the transparency. If an overhead is not an option, you can always print out your letter in a larger format and trace your handmade template.

3 Holding your MDF or wood steady, carefully trace your letter onto your piece. Once your letter is drawn, using your secondary color and your smaller paintbrush, fill in your letter.

When your letter is nearly dry (learning the perfect moment comes with practice) gently wipe away the paint in the center with a rag or paper towel.

If you take too much away, you can always fill in a few areas with paint and do it again. Sometimes layers are fun with these as well.

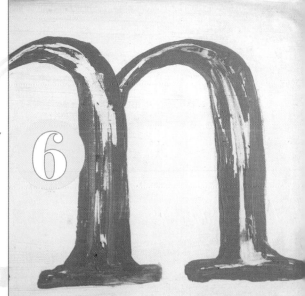

5 Once your letter is dry, apply your stain from the outside in. Wiping as you go, simply remove as much as possible with a paper towel or cloth.

This gives your letter an antiqued look, for that tea-stain finish we love, and adds some timeless character.

Step back and enjoy . . . You're done!

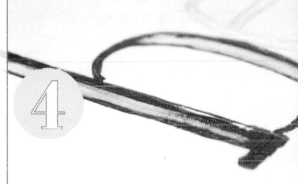

the Edith letter

1 Edith makes a beautiful creation for any space. The same concept can be used to create sentences as well. This makes a great little keepsake for leaning, or hanging in a collection of various pieces.

2 Painting and taking away layers can build a timeworn, classic look. Consider coating the sides in the same secondary color as your focal color for a look of added dimension on the walls. Don't worry about any stray pencil marks when you finish tracing your letter. Simply use your base paint when you come back to touch up any mistakes before you stain.

3 The paint colors used here include Behr's Adriatic Mist, Benjamin Moore's Chantilly Lace, Grandfather Clock Brown, and Silver Satin. On the walls: Behr's Irish Mist + Benjamin Moore's Robin's Egg Blue.

Emerson

Mia

A timeless, vintage, personalized feel for any space in need of that handmade touch.

Emerson Lilly

A sweet idea for any space lacking a little personalization, this frame will certainly perk up the walls.

Stemming from the idea of Edith, these name plaques are a natural extension to combine and create a wonderful look for any space.

No cutting required, these MDF and trim combos become a great team for making something more. Handcrafted letters and pretty layers of paint possess an understated elegance.

Trim and paint add a special touch to that vintage feel.

A stunning creation for any space, these handmade name plaques have a timeless feel.

Mia

difficulty	time	price
1	2	$

Perfect for nurseries or that special little space, this great, not-so-small name plaque is the perfect addition to any wall.

the **Mia** name plaque

breaking it down:

> Materials

MDF and Wood + Trim Cut to Size
Any MDF, wood, or trim cut to size. This is based on your preference.

Overhead Projector + Transparency

Paper Towels or Rag

Paintbrushes

Wood Glue + Hot Glue

Tips + Tricks

* You can have your MDF and trim of choice cut to size at your local hardware store. No cutting required!

* When you place your trim, use a combination of hot and wood glue to secure it for the short term while the wood glue dries.

* We recommend using a projector and transparency with this project. It produces one-of-a-kind results with your fonts.

* An alternative to a projector would be finding letters to use as a template. A great solution for this is printing and cutting them out one by one.

* You can use the same process as Edith to wipe away paint and age the letters, or add a lighter version of the paint in various areas on top to give it a multidimensional appearance.

* Fonts used here: Dalliance + Filosofia.

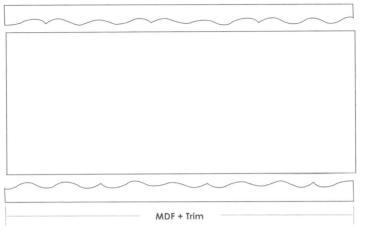

MDF + Trim

What keeps Mia so simple is the no-cutting approach to perfecting handmade walls. Simply have the MDF and your trim of choice cut to size (remember, the local hardware store will perform these outside cuts for you).

Glue the trim to the top and bottom. Use both wood and hot glue to secure it while it dries so you may continue to work on it, if needed.

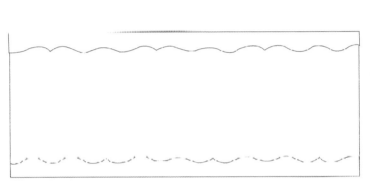

This is where your hot glue combined with wood glue comes in handy. While the wood is stabilized and drying, apply a few coats of paint.

Again, we enjoy older paint for this treatment, so if you've been looking for an excuse to use your gloopy, leftover paint in the garage, the time is now. Fill in all the seams where the trim connects to the MDF, for one continuous aged look.

Emerson Lilly

Once those first base coats have dried, break out your stencil or overhead projector. Trace and paint.

Waiting until your letters are almost dry, distress your wording a bit for more of an aged interest, if you wish.

When all of these are dry, apply your stain in stages from the outside in. Place it a bit heavier around the edges and in creases for a timeless, classic, vintage look.

margaret
catherine

Emerson Lilly

the Mia name plaque

1 Mia is a beautiful, understated addition to any room. This artwork makes a great one-of-a-kind gift and adornment for your handmade walls and spaces.

2 Mia makes a simple project that can be completed in just a few hours. Placing your trim and initial coat of paint makes it easier to center the wording on the plaque.

3 As a general rule of thumb for the best look on these name plaques, always place your type a bit higher, slightly off dead center, for a lighter look on the walls.

8.10.02

Oliver

Oliver is a great display for all things names, numbers, and everything in between.

Oliver gives the illusion of a timeworn piece ripped right from the hinges of your favorite antique store. Personalized by you, it will have a genuine meaning that money just can't buy.

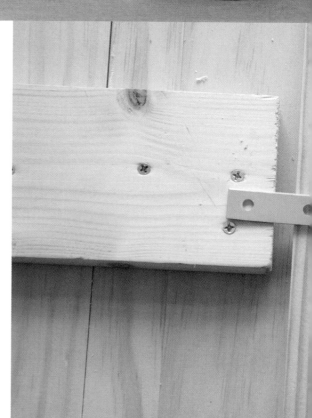

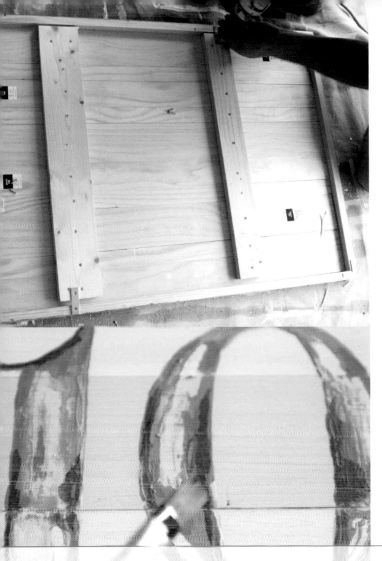

A sentimental soul, Oliver combines a variety of shapes and sizes to form a diverse sign for your home.

Looking as though rescued from the hinges of one of those great little antiquated stores, this old soul proudly displays something personal just for you. From wedding anniversaries to addresses, or even a combination of ideas, the possibilities are endless because each creation by you will be unique and completely different. Pick a day . . . Any day . . . Name or number, for that matter. Oliver makes a great display for your home.

A handmade plaque for one-of-a-kind memories.

Built from a combination of planks in various sizes, Oliver combines paint, stain, and contrast in both color and size. Utilizing the same concept as Edith, with the rubbed older look of paint on boards, Oliver is a beautiful piece for any space.

Oliver

difficulty	time	price
2	2	$

The ultimate way to commemorate a special occasion or memory, Oliver is a great display for days gone by.

the Oliver plaque

breaking it down:

Materials

1 × 2 × 6 Wood (4)

1 × 3 × 6 Wood (2)

1 × 4 × 6 Wood (2)

Box of #6 • 1¼-Inch Screws

Corner Brackets (4)

Flat Joining Brackets (4)

Sandpaper

Wood Glue

Projector + Transparency or Cut Template

Paint + Stain of Your Choice

Tips + Tricks

Always remember that your handy-dandy local hardware store will be more than happy to cut the original pieces for you, for free. Simply starting out with the purchased piece at the right size is an easy beginning.

When laying out all your pieces together, brace them against a straight edge such as a wall to make sure all your pieces are straight.

Do the same thing when screwing in your back braces to keep those edges straight and at a right angle.

For this particular set of numbers, we used the font Otama and layers of paint with the same process we used in Edith. The colors layered were as follows: yellow, gray, blue, green (wiped away in between each layer). We applied stain with a paintbrush on the very top for an aged, timeless feel.

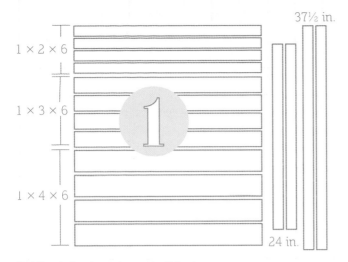

1×2×6

1×3×6

1×4×6

37½ in.

24 in.

Cut the following pieces to 3 feet:

1 × 2 × 6 (four)
1 × 3 × 6 (four)
1 × 4 × 6 (four)

Cut one of the remaining 1 × 2 × 6 pieces into 24 inches and 37½ inches, then cut the other one the same way.

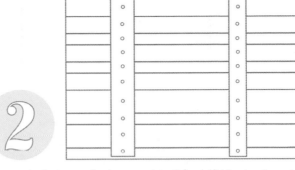

Lay out all pieces that are cut to 3 feet (36 inches) and set aside one of each of the 1 × 3 and 1 × 4 pieces. Arrange the rest of the pieces in the order you would like them to go. With the other ten pieces lying face down, cut the remaining 1 × 3 and 1 × 4 to 24 inches. Attach the two pieces by screwing them to the back of these planks, at 12 inches in from each end. These are your braces.

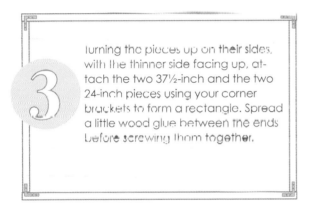

Turning the pieces up on their sides, with the thinner side facing up, attach the two 37½-inch and the two 24-inch pieces using your corner brackets to form a rectangle. Spread a little wood glue between the ends before screwing them together.

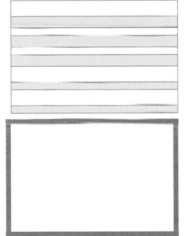

Stain or paint the two built pieces to your desired finish. As always, if you choose to stain, use wood conditioner first.

For our piece, we chose to alternate Benjamin Moore's Wedgewood Gray + Chantilly Lace and then add a touch of stain on each plank. We rubbed these pieces down with a rag for that old tea-stained look, and then went back with a paintbrush in between each plank for a stronger definition in between.

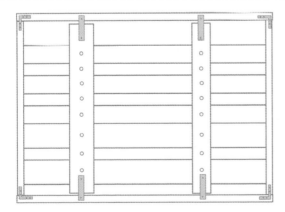

Once both pieces are dry, with the piece in step two lying face down, slide the rectangle from step three over the top of it.

Connect the pieces using your flat brackets on the edges. Spread a little wood glue between the ends before screwing them together.

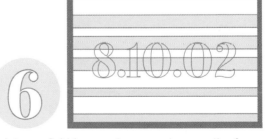

Paint your finishing quote or numbers on the face of the plaque. For our example we used the font Otama, and the same aging process used in the Edith letters. We simply wiped away in between each layer when it was nearly dry. We topped it off with stain on a paintbrush adding emphasis around the edges. To achieve this look, you can use a projector and a transparency or a hand-cut template from a printer. Just make sure your numbers or lettering are straight! Trace, paint, and you're done.

the Oliver plaque

1 Oliver is a great creation to display your fondest memories in style. From addresses to anniversaries, this beauty is personalized by you.

2 There will be gaps in between your wood. But the beauty is found in the rustic imperfections.

3 Make sure you use the process of staining to your advantage. Rub it on and off, and then emphasize the gaps with a separate paintbrush.

4 To achieve the look seen here, we used layers of paint on top of the planks and wiped away each layer as we went. Yellow, gray, green, blue, and then edges of darker stain on top of that final painted number for a super aged look.

5 If you choose to stain, we recommend using wood conditioner to avoid future splotching. You can also combine the stain and painterly look for a new and old kind of combination.

6 In lieu of a projector and transparency, remember that printing in a larger format and cutting out your own numbers or letters is always a viable option. Just make sure your artwork is straight before your transfer, no matter what your method.

Archer

The most complex design in this book, with two options for composition, is Archer. This makes a striking piece with quite the rewarding outcome.

Striking features
and beautiful
finishes create
this incredible
treasure for
your home.

With an interesting combination and contrast of stains and paint, layers and texture, Archer is a sight to behold and a real statement-maker on any wall.

Whether made of MDF and beautiful layers, or wood with pretty punchy colors, the possibilities for Archer practically run the gamut.

A nod to vintage Americana.

Archer carries that old Route 66, campy all-American feel. This is the perfect accessory whether your space is styled to the hilt for little boys galore or a simple one-of-a-kind unexpected finish for your handmade walls. It's this unique look that makes Archer a stunning creation for the home.

Archer

difficulty	time	price
5	4	$

Archer is that classic, striking wall piece that lends to the look of retro Americana and Route 66. A great piece for any space.

the Archer arrow

breaking it down:

> Materials

1 × 6 × 6 Wood (1)

1 × 2 × 6 Wood (6)

Miter Box or Saw

Box of #6 • 1¼-Inch Screws

Wood Glue

Stain or Paint of Your Choice

There are two versions for Archer: Simple MDF, which includes the basic shape, or a more detailed version with many planks joined together. One is with the traceable template included in this book and the other is created with layers of wood. The option you choose and level of difficulty is up to you.

Tips + Tricks

We have two options for Archer. One can be traced, cut, and painted from the template included. This is the simpler version. Just visit our website for that template: *www.thehandmadehome.net/files/archer.pdf*. The other option is one composed of planks, following the directions included in these plans.

For the MDF version: Simply trace onto a sheet of MDF and cut. We added layers of paint to create a dimensional feel to this version of Archer, as well.

As you cut your pieces, number them on the back and keep them organized in their categories so that later on you will know where each piece goes.

For extra support, spread some wood glue on the 1 × 6 and 1 × 2 braces before attaching them.

1

Cut the following 1 × 2 sizes for the top portion (front of the arrow):

19½ in.

15 in.

10½ in.

5½ in.

3 in.

For the mid section of the arrow:

16 @ 7 in.

For the back braces: Top portion

3 in.

For the bottom portion of the arrow:

10 @ 13¾ in.

12⅛ in.

9⅛ in.

For the back braces: Bottom portion

11 in.

5½ in.

Also cut a 1 × 6 × 6 down to 45 inches for the middle brace on the back

1 × 6 × 6 @ 45 in.

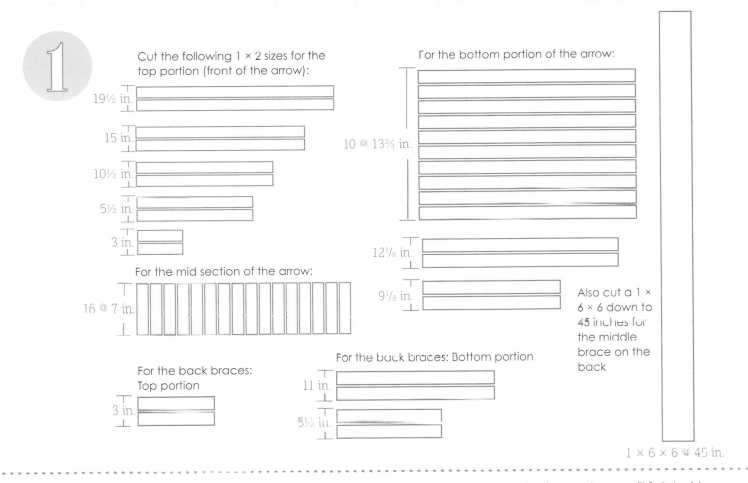

2

Using your 1 × 2 × 6's, cut the pieces using the following specifications. To make these cuts, you will first decide which will be the top and which will be the bottom of your board. Measure in the appropriate length on both ends. Place a mark and draw a line with a straightedge. Once you have the line, you will cut your piece. At this point, we recommend labeling your pieces of wood (on the back) and staying organized as you cut. It will feel less like a puzzle once you have them all placed.

a measuring in as the illustration shows, cut to the corner

1¹⁵/₁₆ in.   2⅜ in.

19½ in.

These planks are for the top (arrow head) portion of your arrow. Measure in equally on both ends of the board while following these measurements.

19½ inch (two): Measure in 1¹⁵/₁₆ inches on one side + 2⅜ inches on the other side
15 inch (two): Measure in 1¹⁵/₁₆ inches on one side + 2⅜ inches on the other side
10½ inch (two): Measure in 1¹⁵/₁₆ inches on one side + 2¾ inches on the other side
5½ inch (two): Measure in 1¹⁵/₁₆ inches on one side + 1⅛ inches on the other side

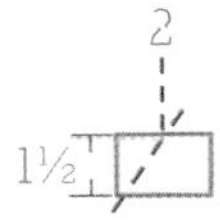

2

1½   For the two 3-inch pieces you've cut, measure the length to 2 inches and cut outward to the bottom corner.

b

1½ in.   1½ in.

9⅛ in.

measuring in as the illustration shows, cut to the corner

These are for the tail, or bottom portion of the arrow.

9⅛ inch (two): Measure in 1½ inches on both sides
12⅛ inch (two): Measure in 1½ inches on both sides

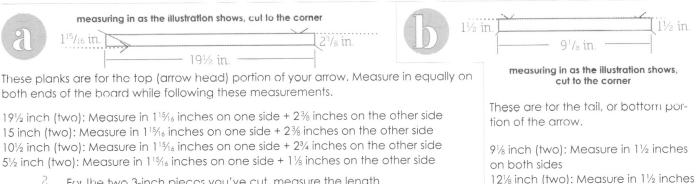

You're almost there. This last step is a bit easier because once you get one right, you can simply repeat the final steps again and again.

For these pieces, you will measure in a different manner, because the angles on each end will be going in opposite directions. So again determine a top and bottom of each piece of wood, and also determine a right and a left. You will measure in from the top left and the bottom right and place a mark, draw your line, and cut as above.

13¾ inch (ten): Measure in from the top left 1½ inches. Measure in from the bottom right 1⅛ inches.

c

measuring in as the illustration shows, cut to the corner

1½ in.   1⅛ in.

13¾ in.

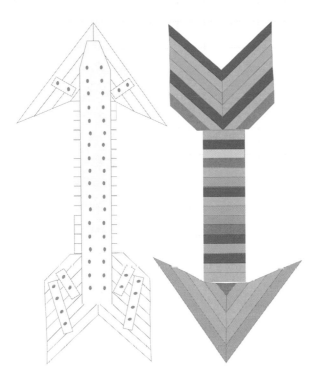

3

Sand all the ends of your newly cut pieces. Using the numbers on the back, line the pieces up and lay them face down. Make sure they are snug and fit nicely together. Lay your 1 × 6 on top and trim any excess off. Once trimmed, begin attaching the 1 × 6 to the cut 1 × 2 pieces with your screwdriver. We suggest starting with the middle pieces. Once they are all screwed to the 1 × 6, use the remaining 1 × 2's that you cut for braces to brace the appropriate areas. (Top portion braces: two 3-inch; bottom portion braces: two 5½-inch + two 11-inch.)

Once you're finito: The main look you see was completed by staining the entire piece, and then lightly painting separate planks with alternating colors. To take it to the 'whitewashed look' simply continue painting, and rub a thin layer of white paint in varying thicknesses on each plank, then wipe away.

the Archer arrow

1 Archer is a complicated process with a lot of steps. This is why we included an MDF alternative. Simply visit our site at www.thehandmadehome.net/files/archer.pdf to download and print onto a transparency. Using your projector, trace it onto MDF, cut, and paint to your desired look.

2 The look that you see on our MDF version is created using a blue paint base, then white in various places. After that, the arrow was taped off and stripes were established. From there, because it was latex paint, we simply scraped, peeled, and distressed our way in various areas for that finished, old, fun look. The best way to peel back those layers? A butter knife.

3 For the multiplanked version of Archer, we waited until the planks were assembled and then stained the entire arrow. Choosing various colors, we added color to different planks as we went.

4 One step further would be the arrow with the whitewashed technique. We added even more color from there, and then layers of white on top of each one for an aged, eclectic feel.

form. follows
functional

{ *chapter* four }

form follows
functional

Functional.

Functional is like a double win in the world of handmade walls. Something that also serves a purpose is like a double whammy, if you will, in the land of limited space. Beyond frames and pretty pieces of art these are the creations that reflect light, tell time, organize, display, and go a little beyond that, as well. Not only are they pretty but, as they say, form follows function. We're not sure which came first in these fun designs, the chicken or the egg.

Each creation is an *extension of you.* **With each piece you create, you make your home yours.**

Claire

Another springboard from the original Edith letters, Claire's design takes the idea to another level.

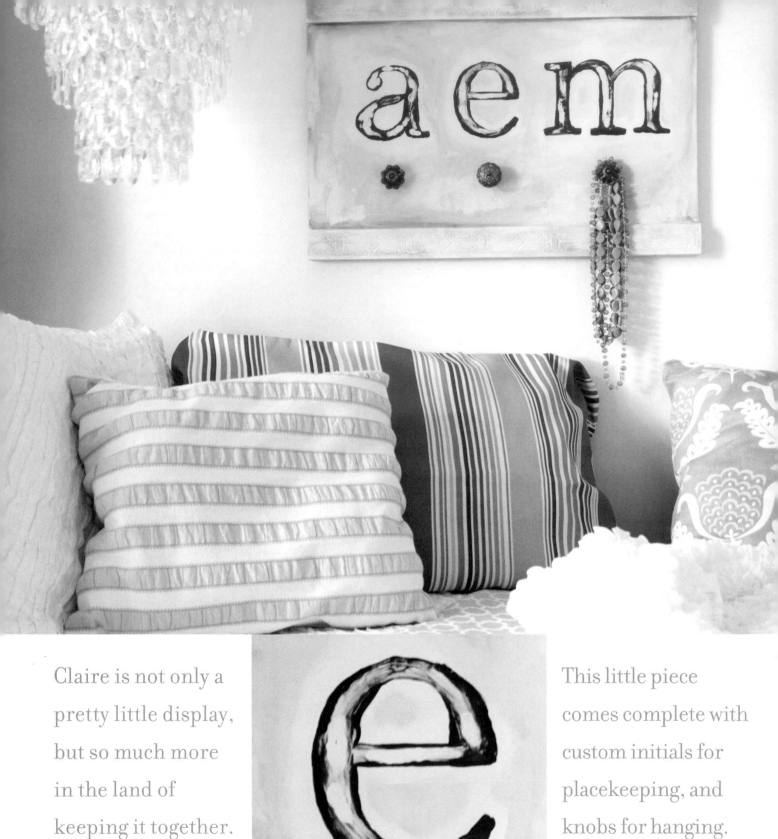

Claire is not only a pretty little display, but so much more in the land of keeping it together.

This little piece comes complete with custom initials for placekeeping, and knobs for hanging.

Switching gears from complex designs back to simple, Claire is a pretty, basic creation that can literally help us find all those easy-to-lose little things. This can be used for holding your smallest treasures, hanging your towels to dry, and finding those perpetually lost keys. An area for hanging makes a pretty little statement on the wall, and a great functioning piece, to boot.

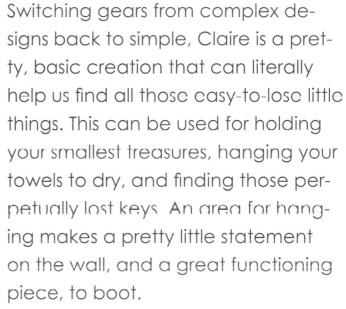

A pretty piece meets functionality in this little organizer.

A bit of a springboard from Edith's letters, Claire is suddenly a functional version for placekeeping. Claire is the embodiment of a place for everything and everything in its place.

With all the different versions of paint and trim, its design is limitless.

Claire

difficulty	time	price
1	**2**	**$**

As a great one-of-a-kind organizer for your wall, not only is Claire pretty; this little piece serves a great purpose.

the Claire display

breaking it down:

▷ Materials

MDF (Cut to Size)

Trim (Cut to Size)

Hardware (Simple Drawer Knobs)

Drill

Dremel

Wood + Hot Glue

Projector + Transparency or Cut Template

Paint + Stain of Your Choice

Tips + Tricks

*Always remember that your handy-dandy local hardware store will be more than happy to cut the original piece for you, for free. Simply starting out with the purchased piece at the right size is an easy beginning.

*Once you screw in your hardware, you'll find that no matter how thick your MDF, there will be a bit of leftover on the back of Claire, which can interfere with hanging. Simply secure with a small nut in the back and cut off the remaining portion with a dremel.

*For Claire to be securely hung, we recommend using two picture-hanging kits. This way, it hangs sturdily on the wall and won't tilt with each movement of adding jewelry or other elements.

*Your greatest material for painting? Your fingers. You'll be amazed at how easy it is to paint once you make it happen with those digits.

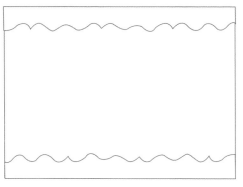

1

Think of Claire in simple terms: A hybrid between Edith + Mia, with a touch of functionality in added knobs. Remember that once you decide on your overall size, whether large or small, your local hardware store helpers can cut both your MDF and trim to the designated size for you.

Once home with your cut pieces, simply join them together with both hot glue (for temporary stability) and wood glue for permanence. When they are nearly dry, apply your first coat of paint. We recommend using older paint for a timeless look with interesting layers.

2

Once your base coat is dry, using either your projector or your template apply your letters. Depending on how many you use, roughly start with the middle letter, and measure from the inside out. Make sure your letters are straight as you transfer them to your piece. We like to eyeball it, but remember to allow room for your hardware, which will be placed below. To err on the side of caution, place your letters a tad bit higher so you have space below for your hardware. Simply trace, and paint.

When the paint is dry, just as you did with Edith start to wipe away (gently with a cloth) the centermost part of each layer. We find that sometimes repeating this gives it an even older, timeworn look.

When this layer is dry and you are happy with your outcome, feel free to give it a light tea stain. Rubbing it off as you go, focusing on the edges, this will add to the older feel.

3

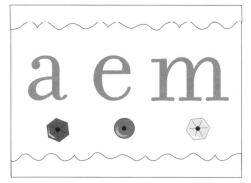

Once your stain has dried, eyeball and drill holes for your hardware. We try to center ours under each letter. Make sure they're straight all the way across with a T-square.

Place the hardware. Once it's secure with a nut on the back, use your dremel tool to trim the screw holding it in. We trim it right to the nut holding it in place so it will hang on the wall nicely.

Hanging tip: Be sure to use two picture-hanging kits so Claire will sit securely on the wall.

the Claire *display*

1. For the fonts in this project, we recommend a classic serif, such as Garamond or Filosofia. Helvetica, however, is always a beautiful choice for a more modern edge.

2. Don't spend too much time measuring or you'll drive yourself batty. It always helps to make sure your letters are straight and placed a little higher to make space for the knobs below. As a general rule in art and design, we always avoid placing things dead center. It should work nicely.

3. We recommend hanging Claire with two picture-hanging kits so that as you add items this piece remains stable. This piece is probably not the best thing for heavy items like bookbags, but if you wanted to use it for that purpose, we recommend you bolt Claire directly into the wall. Supporting it with a stud or wall anchor is always best.

Windsor

This fun clock has a basic
composition, a stunning look . . .
and it can tell time to boot.

Windsor is the culmination of layers of paint, contrasting planks, and splashes of color with dark stain. These come together to make a wonderful statement for any space. This clock is the perfect example of form meeting function, seamlessly.

Telling time is fun again.

Made of MDF cut in a circle with planks of varied stains placed behind it. Simply use our template found on our site here for your number placement: *www.thehandmadehome .net/files/windsorclock.pdf.*

Windsor is quite the unconventional character for your handmade walls. You'll never be late again.

Windsor

difficulty	time	price
3	**3**	**$$**

Windsor is the perfect example of a fun form meeting excellent function.

the Windsor clock

breaking it down:

> Materials

This clock calls for MDF cut to a size 3½ × 3½ feet at ½ inch thick.

1 × 2 × 6 Wood (2)

1 × 3 × 6 Wood (2)

1 × 4 × 6 Wood (2)

Box of #6 • 1¼-Inch Screws

Wood Glue

Clock Hands Kit

Picture-Hanging Kit (Wire)

Skil + Jigsaw

Tips + Tricks

* To make your own version of Windsor, you can use any combination of boards. Just remember that you need to cover 24 inches of space.

* When you purchase a clock hand, make sure to get one that will fit the thickness of the MDF you are using. The shaft needs to be long enough to reach through the hole. We recommend a 1 ³⁄₁₆-inch kit.

* Because of the positioning of the planks behind Windsor, you'll find that the best way to hang this clock on the wall is with a wire picture-hanging kit.

* To trace your numbers, just use our template found on our website. For the best results, once your planks are stained, trace the numbers with a white crayon. The wax from the crayon works nicely over the stain.

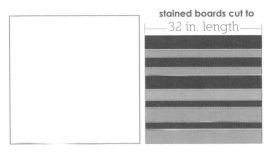

stained boards cut to
32 in. length

Cut your 1 × 2, 1 × 3, and 1 × 4 to 32 inches. You should have ten pieces. Once you trim your wood down, you'll have more and you can use whatever you wish. This is what we chose to use in the thickness department. Cut your MDF to 3½ × 3½ feet. Also go ahead and stain your boards. Do not paint your MDF.

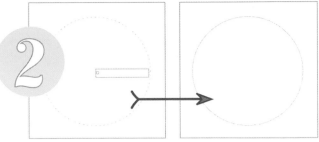

You will need to cut a 2-foot hole in your MDF. Find a scrap piece of 1 × 2 or other lumber lying around. Measure from one side of the plank to 12 inches, and drill a hole at that spot. Next, measure in to the center of your MDF and drill a hole. (This should be at 1 foot and 9 inches.)

Screw the board into the MDF. Place a pencil at the end of the board and rotate the board clockwise, allowing the pencil to draw a perfect circle. Check your line. Then unscrew the board and you are ready to cut.

Use your Skilsaw to start a cut, then finish the cut with your jig saw. Clean the MDF and paint it to the desired finish.

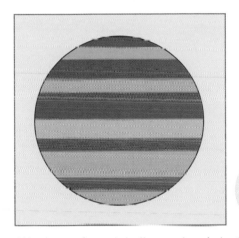

Attach your boards to the center circle. Choose the order you want the boards to go in and place them on the back of the MDF. Once flush and in the right place, begin screwing the boards into the MDF from the back side. Use two screws on each end.

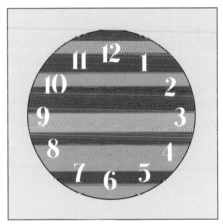

Using the template found on our website (www.thehand madehome.net/ files/windsorclock .pdf), trace (we recommend a white crayon) and paint the numbers on your clock. For a super aged look, leave some of your numbers unpainted in the middle.

On the front side, measure to the center of your circle from the edge of the MDF. It should be exactly 21 inches. Drill a hole slightly larger than the shaft of the clock that you will insert into the hole. Once the hole is drilled, attach your clock device.

the Windsor clock

1 We recommend using whichever width boards you like, as long as they cover the circular area of the clock.

2 Cutting Windsor's center hole is the hardest part about this piece. Drawing the circle can be fun. Getting started with the Skilsaw and finishing up carefully with the jig saw on that line is the key to getting your circle right.

3 To stain your boards at various degrees of finishes, keep going with different coats on each board. It helps to lay out all your wood in the order it will go and start from there.

4 To attain the same finish seen here, we started with a layer of blue topped with splotches of yellow and green. We then added solid and rubbed layers of white. We topped it all off with a light tea stain to seal and give it that timeless look.

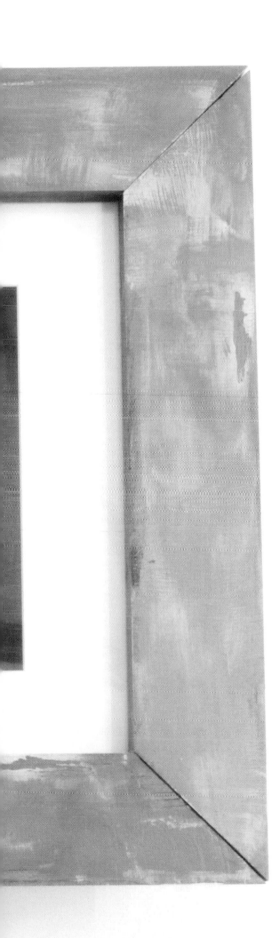

Cooper

The perfect little pocket for your wall, Cooper holds those precious memories on display for all to enjoy.

In a design like Cooper,
more than just memories
are displayed. A moment in
time is created on the wall.

Mass-produced shadow boxes can be expensive, and if we're honest, prettier ones with detail can be nearly impossible to find.

This design establishes a new use for displaying those hard-to-part-with memorabilia and keepsakes.

Something special to display your beautiful memories.

As the creator you can make your own size, choose your own finish, and create a truly unique look for your pretty little displays.

Cooper

difficulty	time	price
3	3	$$

A beautiful display for one-of-a-kind memories.

the Cooper box

breaking it down:

▶ Materials

1 × 2 × 6 Wood (4)

1 × 6 × 8 Wood (1)

Corner Brackets (8)

Plexiglas 16 × 20

MDF 20 × 16

Window Screen Clips (8)

Framing Matte 20 × 16
Available as a standard size in the framing section at most craft stores. (Cut out in the middle 13½ × 10½)

Small Hinges (2)

Magnet

Fabric

Small Package of 1-Inch Finishing Nails

Small Package of 2½-Inch Finishing Nails

Paint + Stain of Your Choice

Miter Saw (or Miter Box + Skilsaw)

Tips + Tricks

✳ Always remember when drilling Plexiglas to hold it down firmly so that it does not run up the drill bit.

✳ In the place of MDF, you could line the back of the shadow box with any other width of planked wood.

✳ Make sure to drill the hole slightly larger than the screw you will be using, when drilling your Plexiglas.

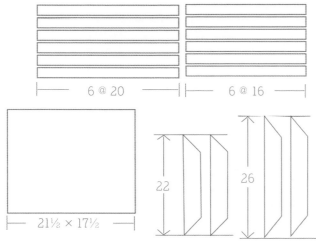

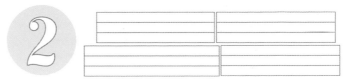

6 @ 20   6 @ 16

21½ × 17½   22   26

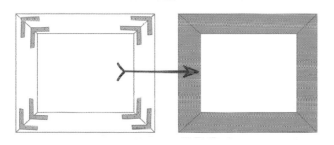

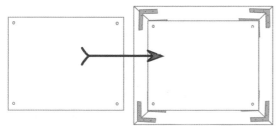

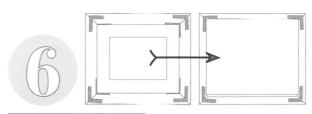

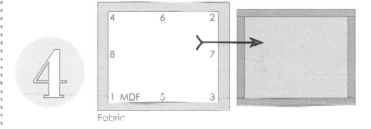

1 Make the following cuts and sand the ends of all pieces. Cut your 1 × 2. You will need six cut to 20 inches and six cut to 16 inches.

Cut your MDF to 20 × 16 inches.

Cut your two 1 × 6 22-inch pieces and two 1 × 6 26-inch pieces. Cut the ends of these pieces to a 45-degree angle. It is probably preferable to go ahead and paint or stain all your pieces.

3 Attach your 1 × 6's that have been cut to a 45-degree angle (two 22-inch and two 26-inch pieces) together by spreading a little wood glue between the ends and securing them with a corner bracket

Two brackets for each corner, eight total.

5 Drill a hole in each corner of the Plexiglas at about ½ inch in. Attach the Plexiglas underneath the wood angled frame you just built using some hot glue.

2 Spread glue on the edge of two 1 × 2's cut to 16 inches and clamp them or simply stack them together. Make sure they are flush on the edges, being careful to wipe up any residue that seeps through. Repeat this with the other two 16-inch pieces, as well as the two sets of two 20-inch pieces.

Allow sufficient drying time according to your product, and drive three equally spaced 2½-inch finishing nails through the sets you just glued.

Then attach a third 1 × 2 of corresponding size to each set using wood glue. Allow it to dry and then drive three more equally spaced 2½-inch finishing nails through the sets. (We prefer to make sure one side isn't showing a nail, so that it has a more finished look. Glue the side that was nailed through, not the side without the nail.)

4 Take your MDF, cut to 20 × 16, and wrap it in the fabric of your choosing. Flip it over face down on top of the fabric (also lying face down). Take each side, one at a time, and adhere it to the back. We recommend hot glue or a staple gun. For a smooth look, alternate each side on opposite ends. (Ex: Upper right corner, lower left corner . . . See numbers above for order example.)

Then using the 1-inch nails, nail it to the 1 × 2 box you have just built, so that the fabric will be seen from the front of your finished piece.

6 Place your matte on the Plexiglas and screw in the window screen clips on the sides. These will hold the matte in place and give it that great multilayered look.

Next, attach the hinges on the outside of the box and on the underneath side of the frame. This depends on your orientation for hanging, but this is what your magnet is for if you change your mind. Once the hinges are on, attach the magnet on the opposite, underneath side of the frame. Be sure to center the magnet.

the Cooper *box*

1 Cooper is made with layers of interest. Planked sides make the side view appealing, and it's topped off with a wonderful distressed frame, Plexiglas, and matte for added dimension.

2 To achieve this same look on the framed portion seen here, we recommend using a stain, then painting the planks gray. Leave a few parts exposed for an aged look. On top of the gray, dry brush a little white in various areas. Then add more of the same gray on top of the white. Finish it off by rubbing on some more of your original stain color. This gives it that great, older, aged look.

3 Cooper hangs nicely with a simple picture-hanging kit attached to the back.

Imogen

This multifaceted
looking glass is the fairest of them all.

The embodiment of the ultimate looking glass is a bold take on a one-of-a-kind creation.

Imogen is a bold piece that demands the attention as the centerpiece of any space. This multifaceted accent reflects light, enlarges any room, and serves as a great mirror with an unexpected finish.

This piece sparkles and shines in ways that will really beautify your space. The great part about it is that no matter the size of your mirrors or your finish, this unique piece is a gorgeous sparkling installment for your walls.

The ultimate looking glass.

Imogen's design is versatile and can be altered for any space. We hope you see this plan as a springboard for your own wonderful ideas. This look really emboldens any room.

Imogen

difficulty · time · price

4 · 4 · $$ $$

A one-of-a-kind looking glass to use as a design. The possibilities are endless.

the Imogen mirror

breaking it down:

> ## Materials

MDF Cut to Size

Your MDF will be cut to 5 × 4. We recommend at least a ½-inch thickness for adequate support on the back.

Trim of Choice

Here we opted for a thicker trim for the feel we wanted. This quickly drove up the price. Please note that this is adjustable.

Individual Mirrors

Our 'mirror ball' design calls for roughly 125 smaller (4-inch × 4-inch) mirrors. Order extra, as some will crack!

Wood Glue

Hot Glue

Liquid Nails

Tips + Tricks

* As it pertains to your cut frame, remember to make sure all cuts are made with the long end being the top side.

* For our design, we decided to stagger the mirrors because the mirrors we purchased were not all precisely the same. This worked nicely for us because we liked the look. If you are not staggering your mirrors, make sure they are exact. If they are off even slightly, it will leave a gap somewhere.

* When building this mirror, make sure you have a safe, low-traffic area for your liquid nails to dry for the next 48 hours (or per the directions on your bottle). If not given the chance to dry properly, your mirrors could slide off and crack.

* Working on a flat surface is ideal, but if you have the time and patience, it may be well worth it to move your mirror to its future location on your wall of choice. We chose to lean ours, but if you can, hang your base MDF first, and then tape each piece as you go to really prevent unnecessary cracking.

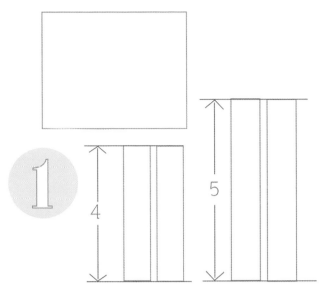

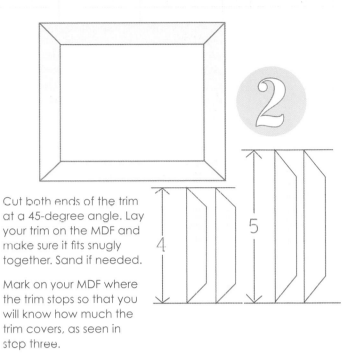

1 Cut your MDF to 5 feet × 4 feet. Your base will be the same size as the frame for support from behind and easy overlapping. Cut two pieces of trim to 5 feet, and another two to 4.

2 Cut both ends of the trim at a 45-degree angle. Lay your trim on the MDF and make sure it fits snugly together. Sand if needed.

Mark on your MDF where the trim stops so that you will know how much the trim covers, as seen in step three.

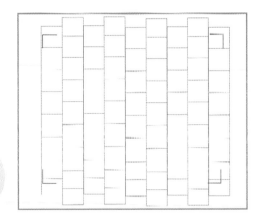

3 Remove the trim and place your mirrors. If you are choosing to stagger your mirrors, you will want to make sure you run all rows over the line that marks where your trim ends. This way you will have something to attach the trim to, as well as cover the entire MDF that will be showing.

Once you decide on the positioning of your mirrors, go through each one row by row, and glue them down individually with the liquid nails.

(If you work from a wall space: Nail your MDF into the wall first, and working mirror by mirror, secure each one individually with tape while it dries. Allow it to dry according to the package.)

4

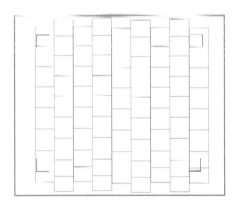

5 As you can see with this project, there aren't many intricate steps you haven't already tried if you've been following the plans in this book. It's simply an issue of patience and finesse with this project. While the mirrors are drying, paint and finish the trim. Because cutting 45-degree angles on a bigger format doesn't always result in perfection, wood filler is your friend. For this frame, we simply painted it and used a contrasting stripe for added interest.

Once it's dry, attach the frame by using liquid nails and a dab of hot glue (for an immediate hold) while the liquid nails dry for that added permanence that you'll need. Check your corner seams on the trim and see if they need to be filled in. If they need to be filled, simply wet and smooth the wood filler once it has been placed. We do both the application and the smoothing with our fingers for a quick, easy process. This is a great way to avoid disturbing your already painted frame with sanding. Once the wood filler is dry, touch it up and top it off with a protective coat of our typical tea stain. This brings definition to all the intricate grooves in this trim's design. Tada! You're finished with your gorgeous creation. Enjoy!

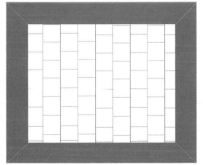

the Imogen mirror

1 When you've completed Imogen, move this frame very carefully to its new location. If you can, simply nail the base MDF into the wall where this new addition will be positioned and create by adding taped mirrors over time. Otherwise, apply the picture-hanging kit BEFORE you start with your mirrors.

2 Place your mirrors in a safe place where they can dry over time. We recommend not moving them for at least 48 hours. Be extremely cautious when moving this project. The mirrors are very fragile but well worth the fun, unique design.

3 For this frame, we used Benjamin Moore's Calypso Blue topped off with a small stripe of Adriatic Mist. We then finished it with a touch of Minwax's Early American, making sure to wipe it heavily into the creases for lots of added character.

tips + tricks
a project reference guide

{ chapter
five }

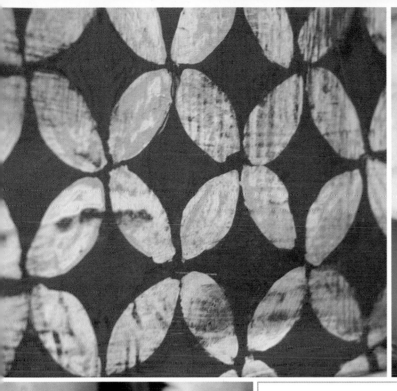

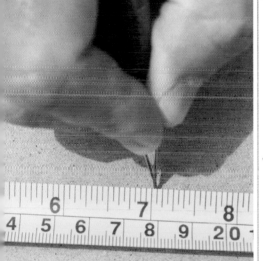

tips + tricks
a project reference guide

Tips + Tricks.

The last chapter of this book is a valuable little guide to check as a reference with all things projects. Here you'll find a few sections chock-full of helpful tips and tricks, from cutting and painting to a full-fledged materials glossary for any of those questions that may be waiting in the wings. We wanted to make it as clear as possible, from step-by-step instructions to illustrated plans and now a few detailed points on how these projects have been created. We hope you find a few interesting snippets here.

If your home is literally a *piece of you ... uniquely yours,* how can you not help but love it?

on Painting

A few tips and tricks on getting just the right look for your finished project.

Just as the process of creating hand-made pieces for your home leaves an impression of yourself behind in each project, you'll find that over time a personal style is developed that you love the most. We believe that in each of us lies an undiscovered artist. No matter how much or little you know about the technicalities of it all, it begins with a little bravery.

A few of our favorite tips + tricks.

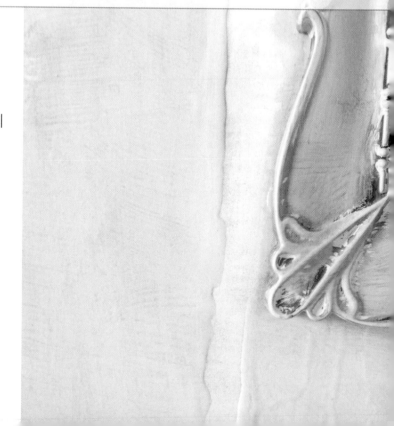

So here, we decided to include a few helpful hints we like to follow for that fabulously perfect, foolproof finish. Every time. On the following pages, you'll find a step-by-step reference to some of the projects you may have spied in the previous chapters. We hope that here, you can use our processes as a springboard for your own. Enjoy!

Don't forget your hands.

With a basic angled brush and a few smaller brushes, a rag for distressing, and your fingers . . . You're an unstoppable painting force. Your hands help you achieve those hard-to-reach angles and distress some areas, as well.

The older, the better.

Most people think the best paint is fresh. We enjoy using your not-so-typical leftover paint for a great layered and aged effect. So break out those old cans sitting in your garage and put them to use! If you have fresh but want a 'crusty' look, try layering your piece with a rough wood filler. It creates an older look.

Side to front.

For basic painting tips pertaining to frames or anything with visible borders: We find it best to paint the sides that secondary (usually darker) color first. Then add your top coat (or lighter color) that will be on the main part of your frame, once the darker color is dry. It keeps the edges clean and neat.

Condition it.

For staining with wood: Always use a wood conditioner. Simply obtain a rag and wipe it over your existing wood. When it's dry, begin your staining process. This prevents future blotchiness and uneven finishes.

It's fun to be distressed.

The fun kind. For the 'distressed' look without using a sander, as seen with Edith and older-looking paint finishes, wait until that paint is almost dry, then pull off the middle by wiping it down the center to achieve that older look. Simply touch up any smudges or boo-boos with your original base coat.

Top it off.

Why do we top off most of our projects with a stain? We love the deeper hues that a tea-stained look can create. It brings out textures and a beautifully classic, deep finish. But best of all, it's our favorite way to protect our creations, without having them scratch or yellow . . . A timeless feel to last for generations.

our favorite paint colors.

We love to use a standard latex paint for our projects in a semigloss finish. Here are a few of our favorite colors. From left to right, top to bottom: Behr's Adriatic Mist, Benjamin Moore's Wedgewood Gray, Calypso Blue, Behr's Asparagus, Benjamin Moore's Once Upon A Time, Behr's Magnolia Blossom, Buttercup, Benjamin Moore's Corn Husk, Silver Satin, Benjamin Moore's Graphite, Chantilly Lace, Behr's Irish Mist, Benjamin Moore's Million Dollar Red, and Minwax's Early American and English Chestnut.

MDF layered with paint.

MDF + base coat + top coat + stain

Whether it's a stencil, stripes, or just a solid coat of paint, the recipe for this look is: 1. MDF (or wood) + 2. A base coat of paint with 3. A top coat (optional; sometimes, more than one color—see the multi stripes) + 4. Finished off with a protective stain. This look can be found in most of our frames with patterns.

MDF and multiple layers.

MDF + base coat + top coat + base coat + stain

An extra step beyond the last one, whether it's a stencil, stripes, or just a solid coat of paint, the recipe for this look is: 1. MDF (or wood) + 2. A base coat of paint + 3. A top coat (optional) + 4. Another layer of base coat + 5. Finished off with a protective stain. This look is found in many of the plans in our art section.

All of the processes that you see in this book can be broken down into five main, basic formulas for creating that one-of-a-kind look. Here, we'll show you how. Simplified with these basic equations, the spectrum of results are endless.

Layered and distressed.

MDF + base coat + top coat + rubbed + base coat + stain

An extra step beyond step two, the recipe for this look is: 1. MDF + 2. A base coat of paint + 3. A top coat (optional) + 4. When that top coat is nearly dry, rubbed and distressed + 5. Another layer of base coat (optional) + 5. Finished off with a protective stain. This look is found on pieces like our clock, letters, and distressed frames.

Simple stain (sometimes, layered).

wood + stain

Sometimes layered, the basic recipe you see here begins with 1. Wood as a base + 2. A stain color of your choice. Whether made of separate planks, stripes, or a solid, simple color, stain can be a great basic treatment for anything. Even stain can be forgiving: Gently scrape away any places that are considered 'bleeding' spots in your finish, especially with stripes. An X-ACTO knife works best. Remember to condition that wood, first!

Stain layered with paint.

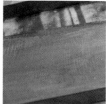

wood + stain + paint + stain

This look begins with: 1. Wood as the base + 2. A coat of stain + 3. Adding on top of that a touch of paint, careful to leave certain areas (like the edges) exposed with only stain. Optional: Top (the gray) with a second color in a lighter tone and go back over it with more of the first paint color + 4. Finally, top it all off with more stain, which darkens and protects the already existing layers. This look is seen on Cooper and Darby.

Following the steps, it's easy to make your own stripes on anything you wish. From frames to textured wall art, all you need is some tape and a little time.

1. Begin by establishing your top coat. Once it's dry, start placing your tape evenly. Use a smaller piece of tape to help with spacing in between.

2. If this is a frame, use a ruler and pencil to connect the corners at a 45-degree angle. Follow that and alternate the colors or connect them on each side.

Painting the best stripes.

3. Working in sections to keep it manageable, once your second coat is nearly dry begin removing middle sections of each stripe to give it that distressed look.

4. If you decide not to do that, you can always use a top coat (the base coat, repeated) on top of the dry stripes. The mottled look is best by rubbing on with your fingers and wiping off. Once dry, top with a light stain.

on Painting

Treat your project as though it's your canvas.

So long, intimidation. There are no rules.

Paint is the most forgiving medium, after all.

Add color with paint and distress a few layers.

Accent the edges with stain for an aged, timeless look..

Be fearless with the everyday materials

to create *extraordinary* results.

WARNING
To reduce the risk of injury, check lower guard. It must close instantly. Hold saw with both hands. Support and clamp work.

AVERTISSEMENT
Pour réduire les risques de blessures. Observe la garde intérieure. Elle doit se fermer instantanément. Tenir la scie à deux mains. Soutenir et bloquer la pièce à couper.

RYOBI

parts away from blade.
result in serious injury.
les parties du corps à l'écart de la lame.
t causer des blessures graves.
las partes del cuerpo alejadas de la hoja.
puede producir lesiones serias.

18.0v

on Cutting

A few of our favorite tips for making cutting (and putting it all together) a little bit easier.

The process of making your own pieces is a lot like the steps to painting. It's easy to be intimidated by tools if you've never used them before. Trust us . . . We've been there.

Simply acquainting yourself with these great, helpful tools will make you more comfortable.

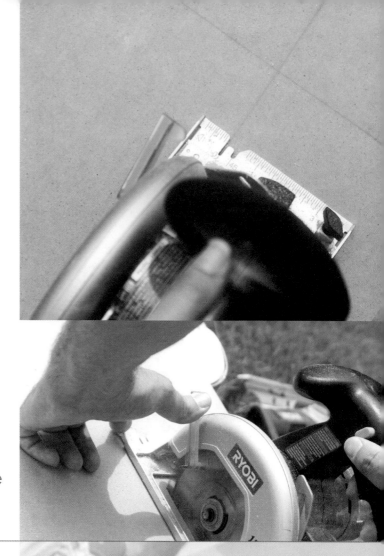

A few of our favorite tips + tricks.

Practicing with everything from the miter to the jig to the Skilsaw will help you gain bravery over time. Remember, we knew nothing and have gradually grown in our knowledge as we practiced more hands-on experience . . . It's the best way to grow your collection and your know-how.

Hot glue!

If you don't want to invest in corner clamps, or any clamps for that matter, try spreading the wood glue on your pieces; then add a drop or two of hot glue, tightly holding the pieces together. The hot glue will dry much faster than the wood glue and give you an instant hold until the wood glue has time to set.

Making it work.

On angled frames, when cutting along a line always remember that if you cut right on the line, you will end up cutting your board a little shorter than you mean to. You have to adjust for the width of your blade. The easiest way to fix this: Always line up your blade on the outside of the line.

Blue is better.

If using a chalk line, always remember to stay away from red. It typically will leave a lasting mark. We prefer to use blue chalk.

Safety first

Remember to always observe all safety precautions when working with power tools of any kind. Be super careful, always.

Stay picky.

Choosing wood might be one of the most important steps in building anything. Take the extra time to check each piece of wood. Check for knots. Is the wood straight all the way down? Is it splintered? The goal: To find as near perfect as you can for the grade of wood you are buying.

No cheating.

You may be tempted to trace one piece of wood on top of another when cutting several pieces the same length. Don't, if you're just beginning in woodworking. While it's okay once in a blue moon, take the extra time to measure it. If you don't you'll be cutting each piece a little long. If you decide you want to save time and trace it, remember that you will probably want to cut on the line instead of cutting on the outside. This is because your measurement will be a tad long because of using a cut piece instead of a tape measure.

It's true.

Remember the old adage about cutting once after you measure twice? True. You can thank us later.

just a few of our very favorite **tools.**

Beyond the basics, some of these may be considered a 'splurge' but here we thought we'd share some items that are well worth the investment once you're ready to take the plunge. From personal experience, these are the products we seriously adore that make creating handmade treasures downright fun. From left to right, top to bottom: miter saw, chalk line, orbit sander, jig saw, carpenter square, and of all things . . . You guessed it. A hot glue gun.

on Cutting

Taking the time to associate yourself with power tools is a lot like taking that first step to finally make your home your own. By familiarizing yourself with the simple processes of cutting, you can easily

become an *expert* in no time.

supplies *glossary*

Apart from the basic materials listed in this book, here you'll find a comprehensive list of tools you'll use to make any of the handmade creations you find here.

Want to know the best part? We've found them all for you. When you visit *www.thehandmadehome.net/project glossary*, you'll find the page on our website where we keep our links fresh and up-to-date. This way, you can read more about each product. It's like shopping, without all the legwork.

Used to make sure that a corner is straight or to draw a straight line off the edge of another straight side.

Carpenter Square

Used to connect two points and form a straight line by popping a string that has chalk on it.

Chalk Line

Clock Hands

Used to hold two pieces together while the glue is drying or while another brace is being screwed in.

Clamp

Used to hold tight two 45-degree angle pieces while the glue is drying or while another brace is being screwed in.

Corner Clamp

A bracket that stands on its own, and is shaped like an L. Used to secure corners. Also known as an L bracket.

Corner Bracket

Great for mounting photos and other artwork for the projects shown in this book.

Perfect for just about anything, especially creating one-of-a-kind patterns.

Double-Sided Tape + Painter's Tape

A flat L-shaped bracket, used to secure corners. Also known as a corner bracket.

Cork Tiles

L Bracket

Used to drill into material. With the right bit, it can also be used to drive screws into material. Drill Bits: Used to drill size-specific holes for screws to fit through.

Can be used in a variety of ways. One of the most important in this book is to saw off metal screws so that a frame or piece of art will hang flush against the wall.

Drill + Drill Bits

Dremel

Handy for a temporary bond while your wood glue dries.

Hot Glue Gun

Great, natural material used for a variety of purposes. Looks fab on Harry.

Jute

Great for securing photos in frames, if you prefer not to use tape.

Photo Corners

Stencils are a beautiful way to finish off any project. And we recommend Royal Design Studio.

Stencil

Used to make finishing or precise cuts. Use this for more control.

A power saw used to make long, straight cuts.

Used to make an angled cut on any piece.

Jig Saw, Skilsaw, + Miter Saw

Tool used in place of a miter saw to achieve an angled cut.

A power sander that has a circular sanding pad.

Mirrors we used for Imogen, and the perfect heavy-duty adhesive for the two materials.

Miter Box   Orbit Sander   Mirror + Liquid Nails

Used to secure a material, yet allows for removal and easy access. Helps keep things on a hinge temporarily closed.

Magnet + Window Screen Clips

Joins pieces and enables one to swing open and closed.

Hinges (Small)

Great for tracing lines, centering frames, and scraping away layers of paint.

T-square + X-ACTO

Perfect for filling any imperfections and seams. No sanding required if you go back with a wet cloth or finger.

Wood Filler

Great, permanent bond for MDF or wood.

Wood Glue

We recommend sawtooth for your everyday needs and wire for projects like Windsor that won't be hanging flush on the wall.

Wire + Sawtooth Picture-Hanging Kits

One investment we couldn't recommend more if you plan on doing a lot of DIY artwork for your homes. Worth every penny!

Projector

We're big fans of Purdy angled brushes because they don't shed (read: drive you bonkers).

We also recommend a small variety of other sizes for various projects that require heavy patterns and painting. These are a great little option for those demands.

Paintbrushes

wrapping it up

When you finally let go, the possibilities are endless.

In the process of creating pieces

for your home, a transformation occurs.

In both you and your lovely abode.

You leave a personal impression . . .

a mark, if you will, on each project.

With each piece, you lose a little fear.

And gain a little bravery.

Each creation is an extension of you.

With every piece you create, you make your home yours.

If your home is literally a *piece of you . . . uniquely yours,* how can you not help but love it?

It's our greatest hope, after looking through this little compilation of ours, that you can use it as a springboard of inspiration. Beautiful homes aren't purchased in one day. They aren't bought 'as a room,' and they aren't thrown together overnight. They probably aren't even held in a collective grandiose round of applause, given their one-of-a-kind unique nature based on who put them together. Maybe one-of-a-kind homes are only appreciated by the creator and those who dwell there. Truly beautiful homes are created over time. They're crafted carefully by an artist who loves to tweak a canvas. They are an honest, illuminating reflection of those who live there. They are beautiful because of the stamp left behind with each little change and movement. The one-of-a-kind, handmade home begins with a desire for something different, as well as the ability to shake off the inhibitions and predetermined ideals of those around us, to forge onward with what we cherish in life. Fearlessly, it begins with the smallest of projects that help us truly pursue what we love. In that, we begin to discover our own abilities from within, reflected in our abodes. It becomes a true celebration of life, by those who live there . . . A beautiful haven, created by you, for the everyday.

about the
authors
the handmade home

Jamin and Ashley Mills began their adventure together as college sweethearts. After a decade of marriage and three offspring later, they currently reside with their family in Montgomery, Alabama. They are the voices behind this book and their website, thehandmadehome.net.

At The Handmade Home, they share their daily journey and down to earth passion as the parents to three incredible children and one crazy dog. In between the mountainous piles of dirty laundry and musical bed fiascos with their glorious little troublemakers, they're also known for their handmade revamps and one-of-a-kind projects as they create a haven for the everyday.

For more inspiring projects and one-of-a-kind creations visit The Handmade Home.

thehandmadehome.net

the end.

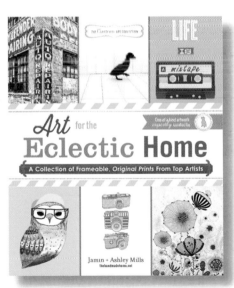